Let it be Simple

journal belongs to...

© 2017 Ranch House Press
All rights reserved. Printed in the United States of America.

www.annettebridges.com

ISBN: 978-1-946371-20-1

Journal Prompts

Let it be Simple

1. If you want to fly, give up everything that weighs you down.
2. What's most important to you? What do you value most? What 4 or 5 things do you most want in your life? Start simplifying with these priorities.
3. Evaluate your time. How do you spend your day? Is what you're doing in line with your priorities? Eliminate the things that aren't and focus on what's most important to you. Redesign your day.
4. Simplify home and work tasks. Focus on the most important and look for ways to eliminate, automate, delegate tasks
5. Not enough hours in the day? STOP doing things that don't matter.
6. Learn to say no. If you can't say no, you will take on too much.
7. Limit your communications. Our lives these days are filled with a vast flow. Begin by scheduling certain times of day and a certain number of minutes with emails, phone calls, etc.
8. Limit your media consumption — TV, Internet, etc. Try a media fast.
9. Purge stuff. Simplify your wardrobe. Edit your rooms, closets and drawers. Eliminate the unnecessary.
10. For the longest time, I thought I needed to be more organized. Now I know I just needed less stuff.
11. Create a simplicity statement. What do you want your simple life to look like?
12. The more you have, the more occupied you are. The less you have, the more free you are.
    ~ Mother Theresa
13. Do what you love with people you love.
14. Stress, anxiety and depression are caused when we are living to please others.
    ~ Paulo Coelho
15. Eat slowly. Slow down to lose weight, improve digestion and enjoy life more.
16. Be present. These two words can make a huge difference in simplifying your life. Living here and now, in the moment, keeps you aware of life, of what is going on around you and within you.
17. Learn what "enough" is. Get off the cycle of more and more by figuring out how much is enough. And then stop when you get there.
18. Create a simple healthy weekly dinner menu. Decide and shop for a week's worth of simple dinners. Find recipes that can be done in 10-15 minutes or less.
19. Have a place for everything. Age-old advice, but it's the best advice for keeping things organized.
20. Find inner simplicity. Spending time with your inner self creates a peaceful simplicity rather than a chaotic confusion. Alone time is necessary for finding out what's important to you.
21. Find a creative outlet for self-expression. We have a need for self-expression and finding a way to do that makes your life much more fulfilling.
22. Simplify your goals. Instead of having half a dozen goals or more, simplify it to one goal at a time.
23. Live life more deliberately. Do every task slowly with ease, paying full attention to what you're doing.
24. Learn to do nothing. Doing nothing can be an art form, and it should be a part of every life.
25. Make a list of your favorite simple pleasures, and sprinkle them throughout your day.
26. Always ask yourself: Will this simplify my life? If the answer is no, reconsider.
27. Simple living frees you to simply live.
28. Live simply and appreciate what you have. Give more. Expect less. ~ Stephen Covey
29. What screws us up most in life is the picture in our head of how it is supposed to be.
30. Sometimes all we need is just a new perspective.
31. Life is simple when you live simply.

color your world

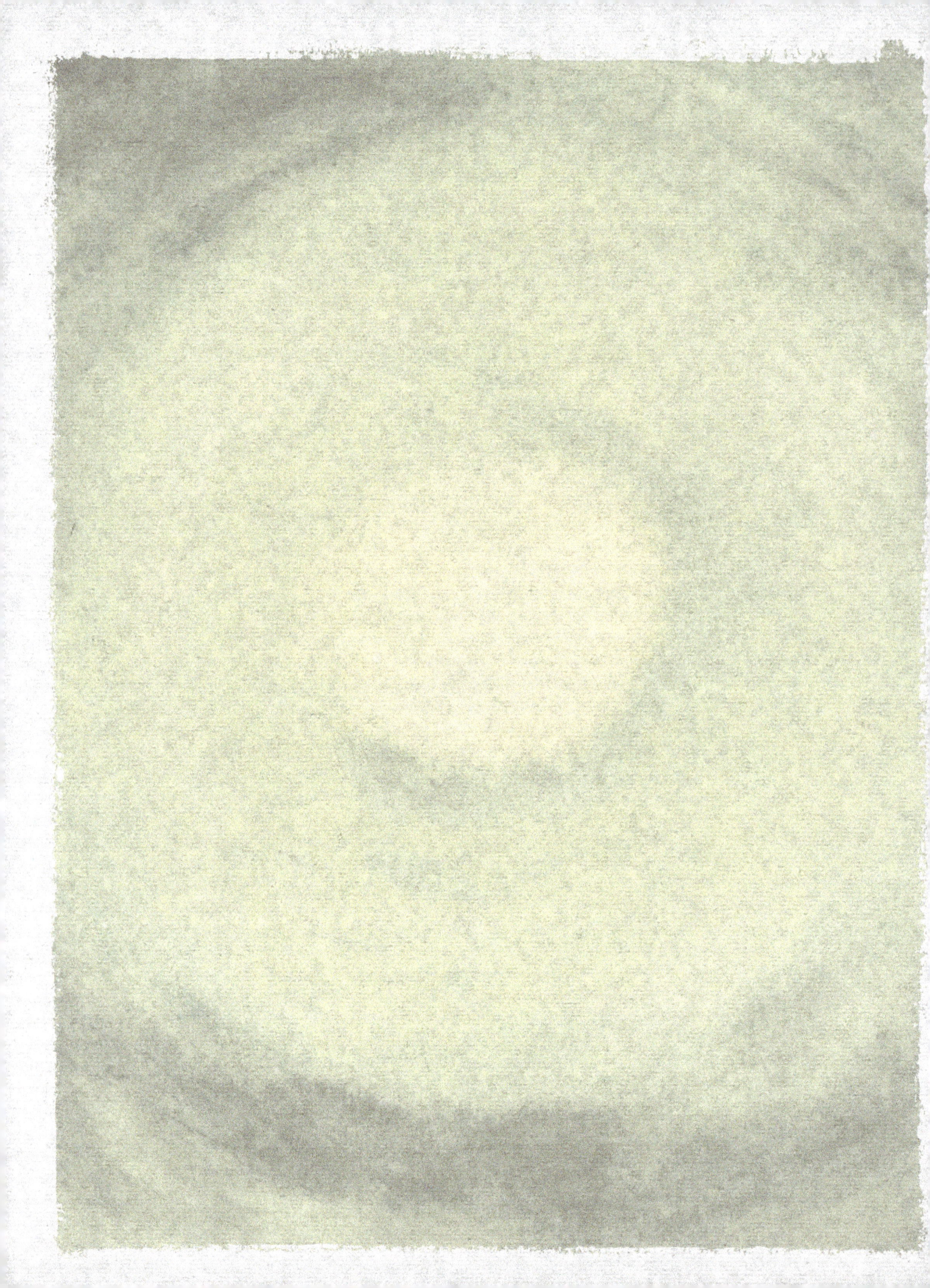

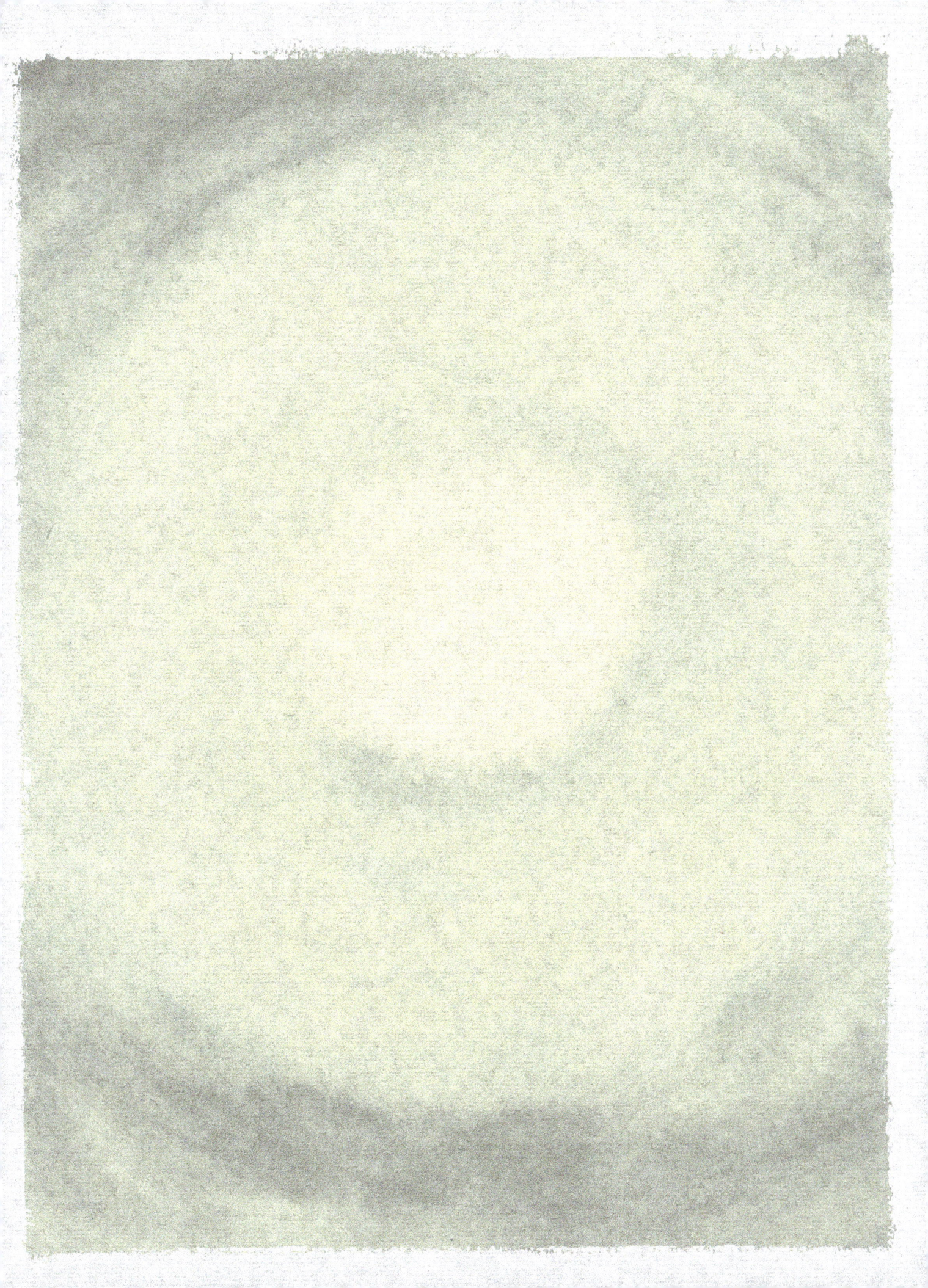

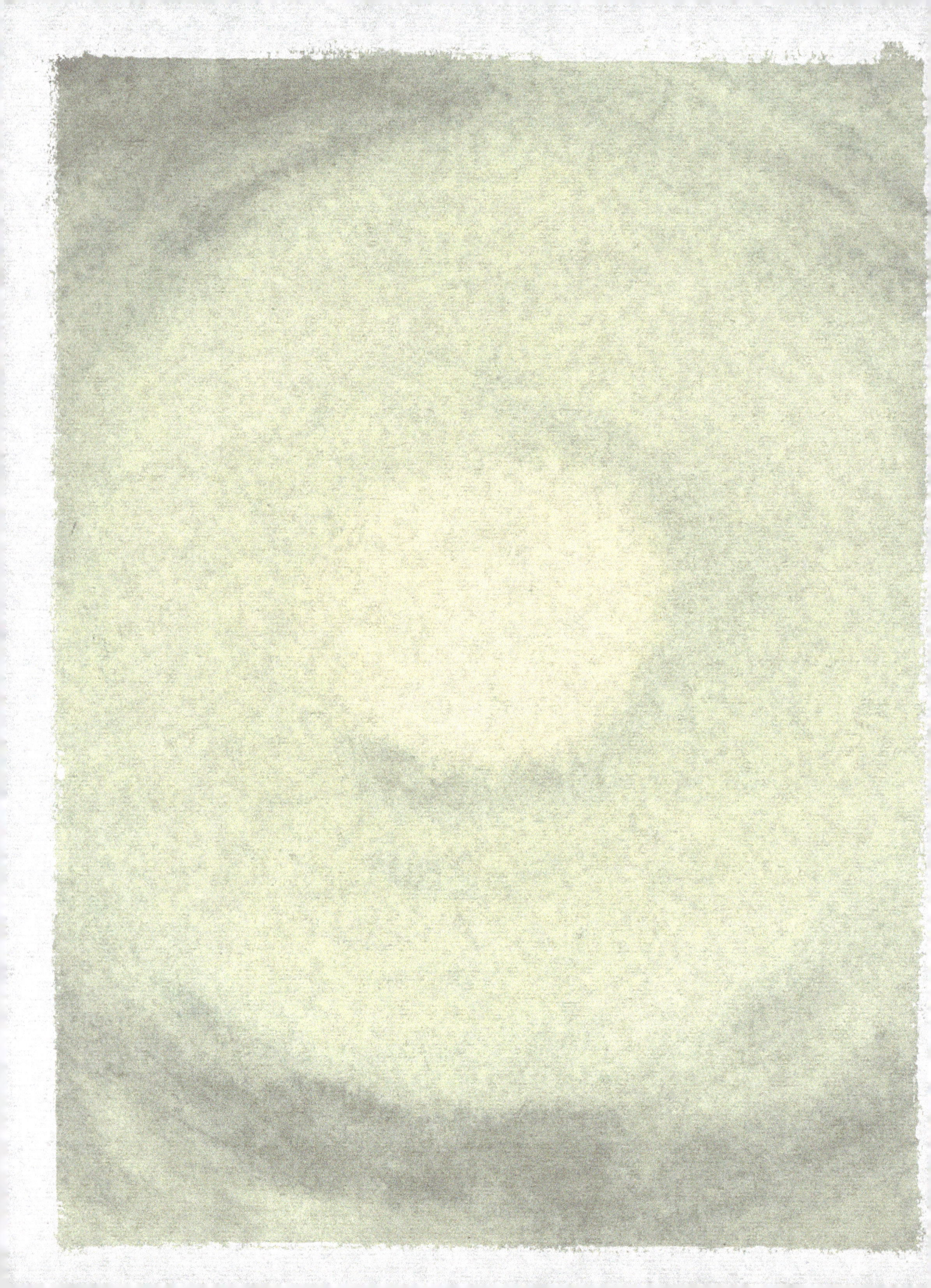

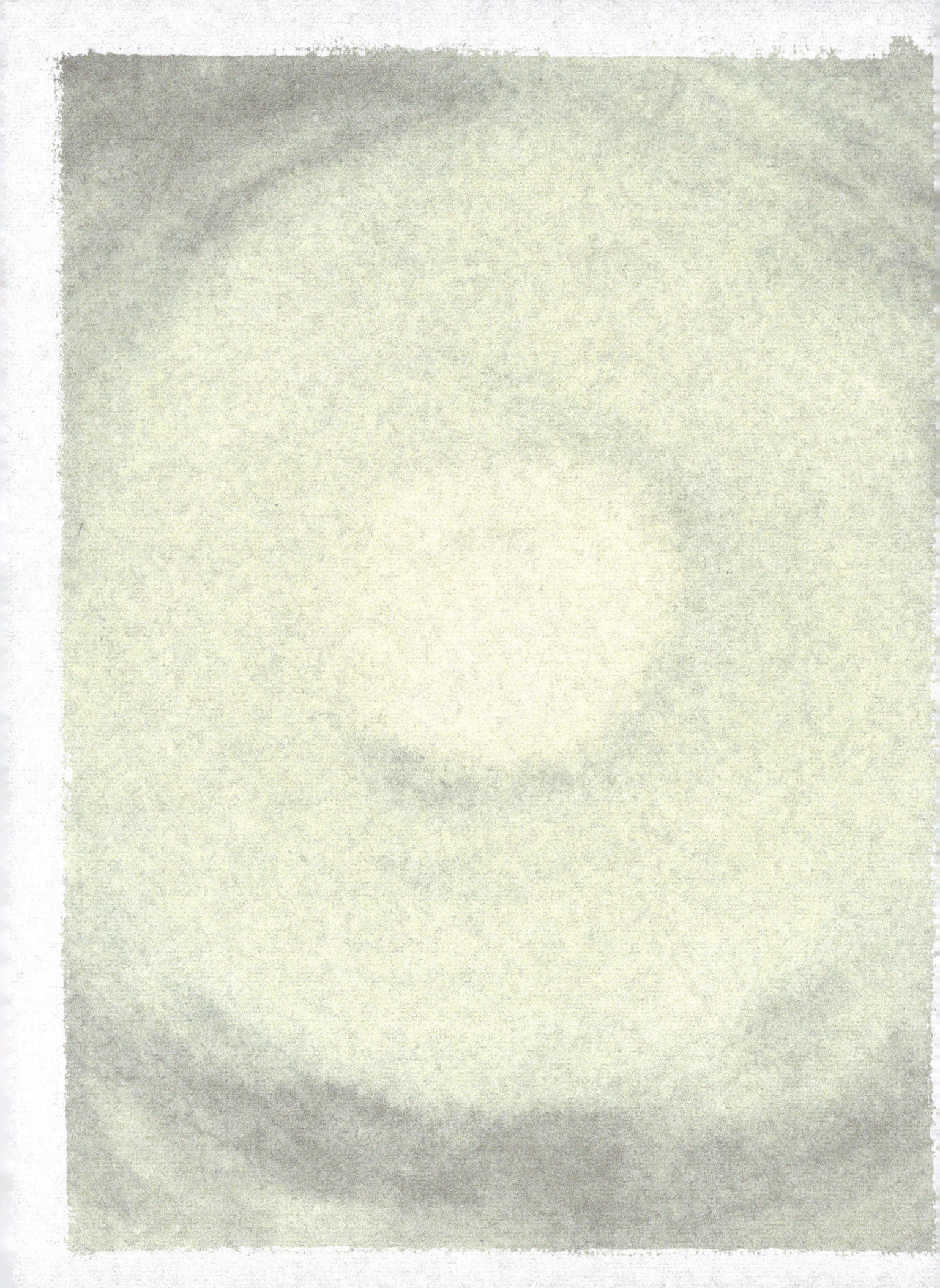

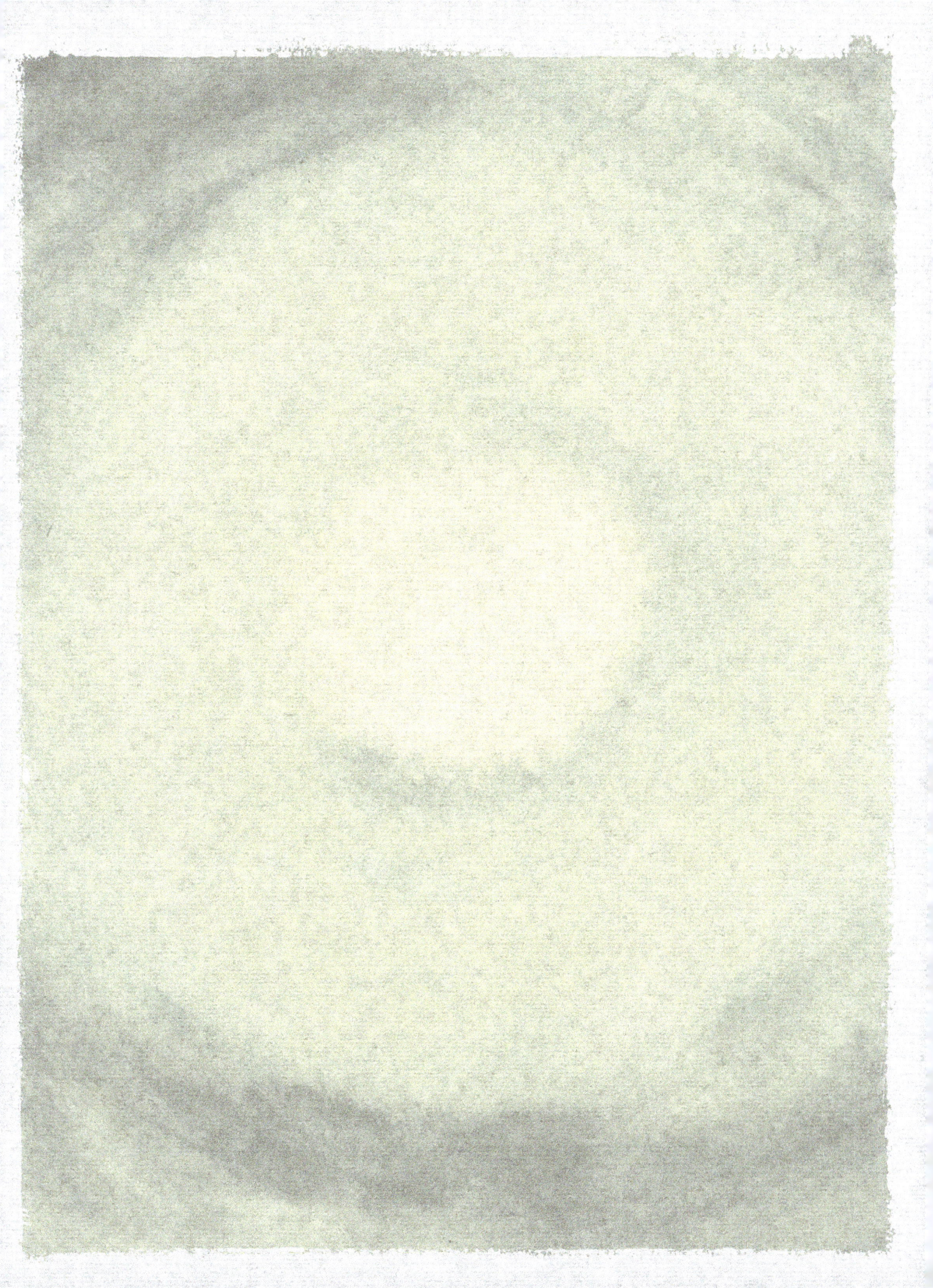

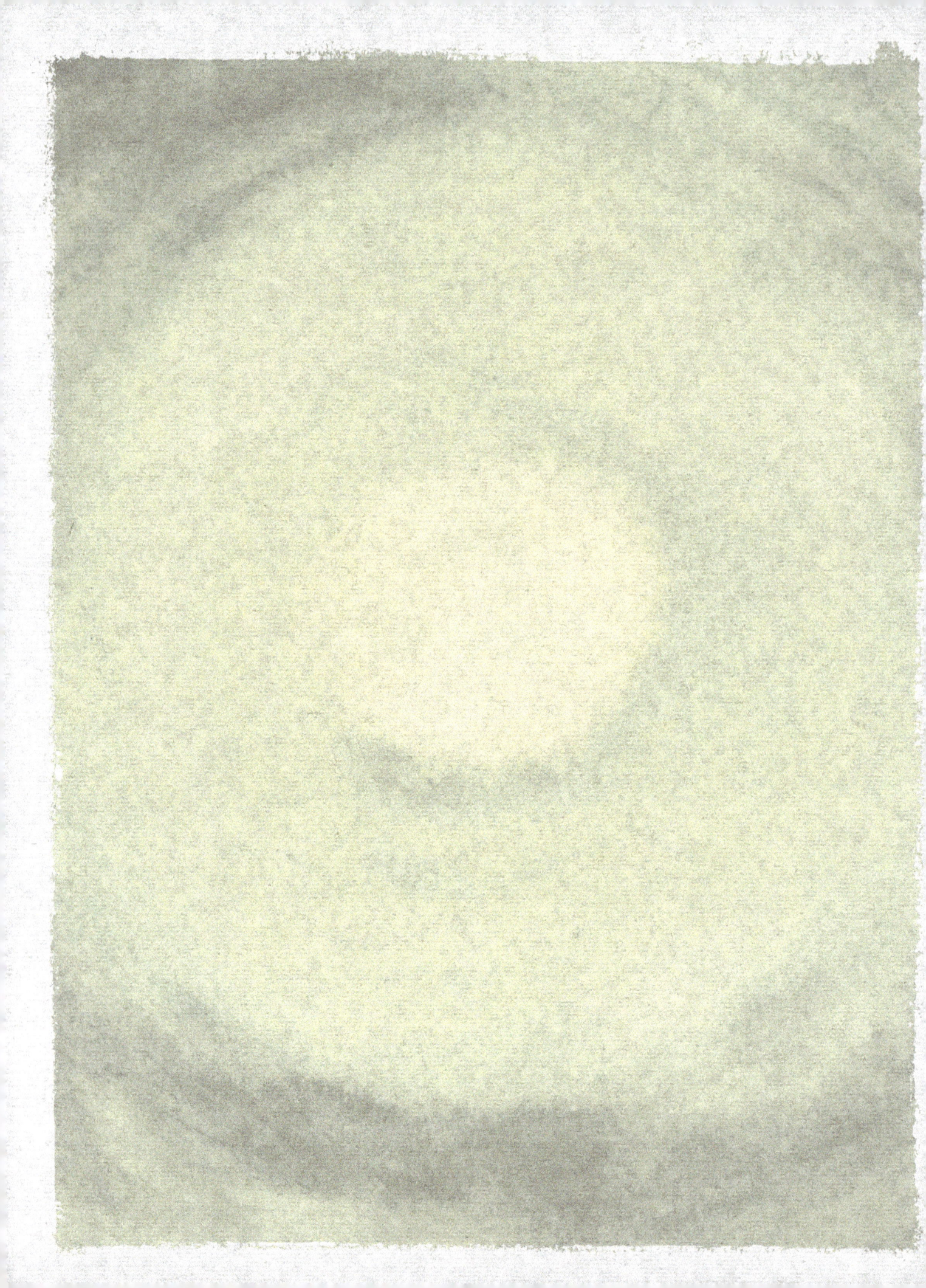

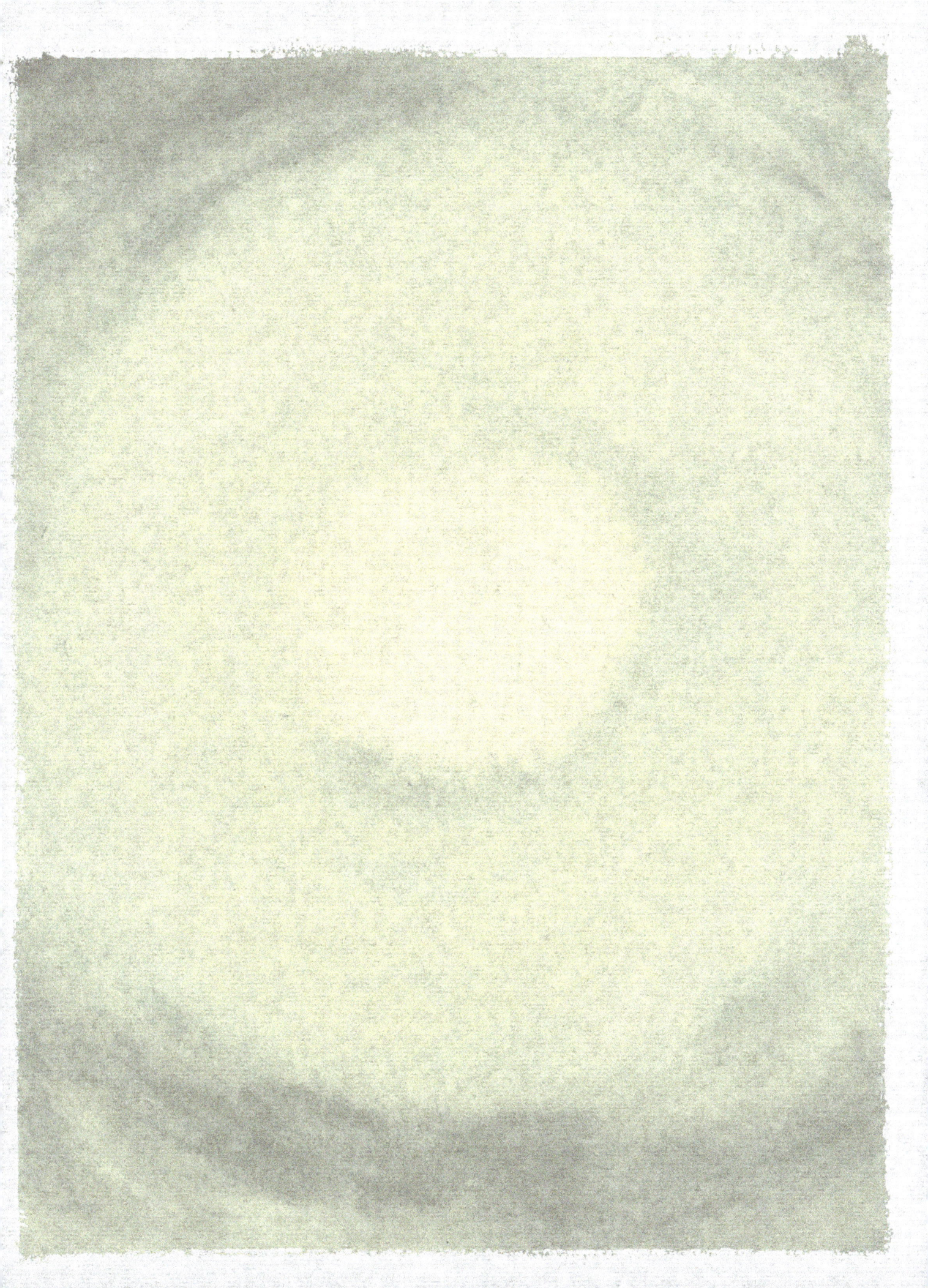

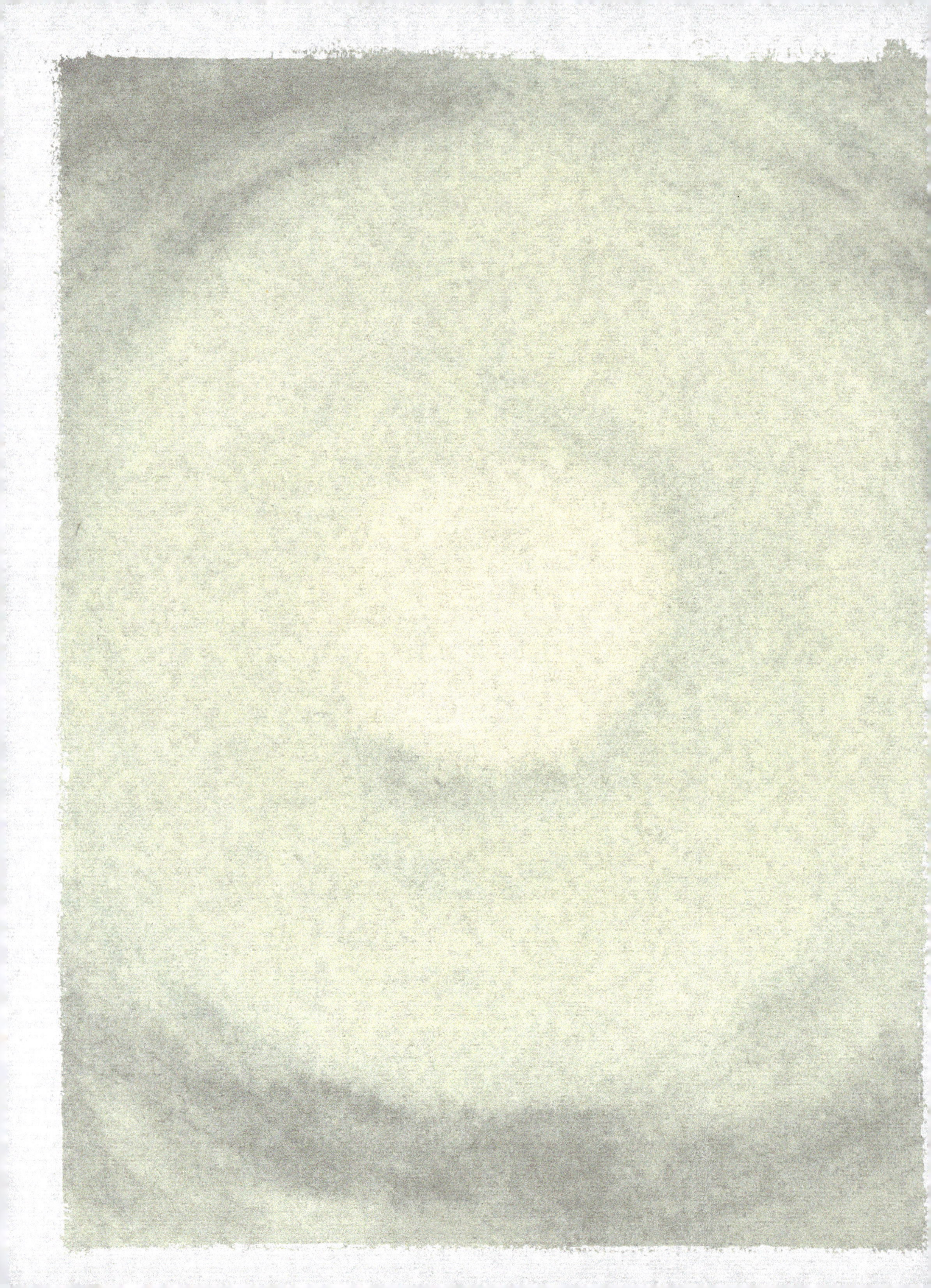

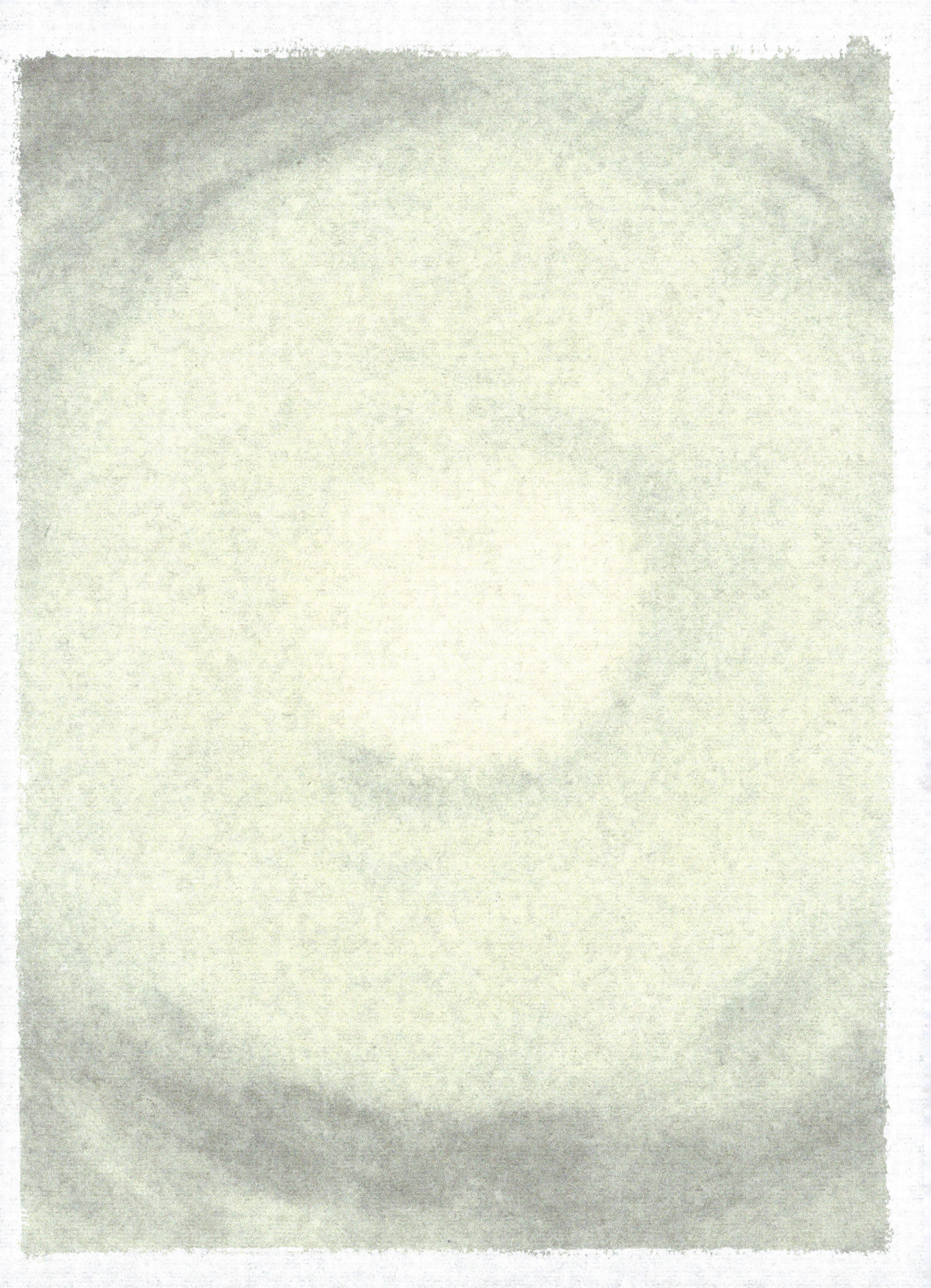

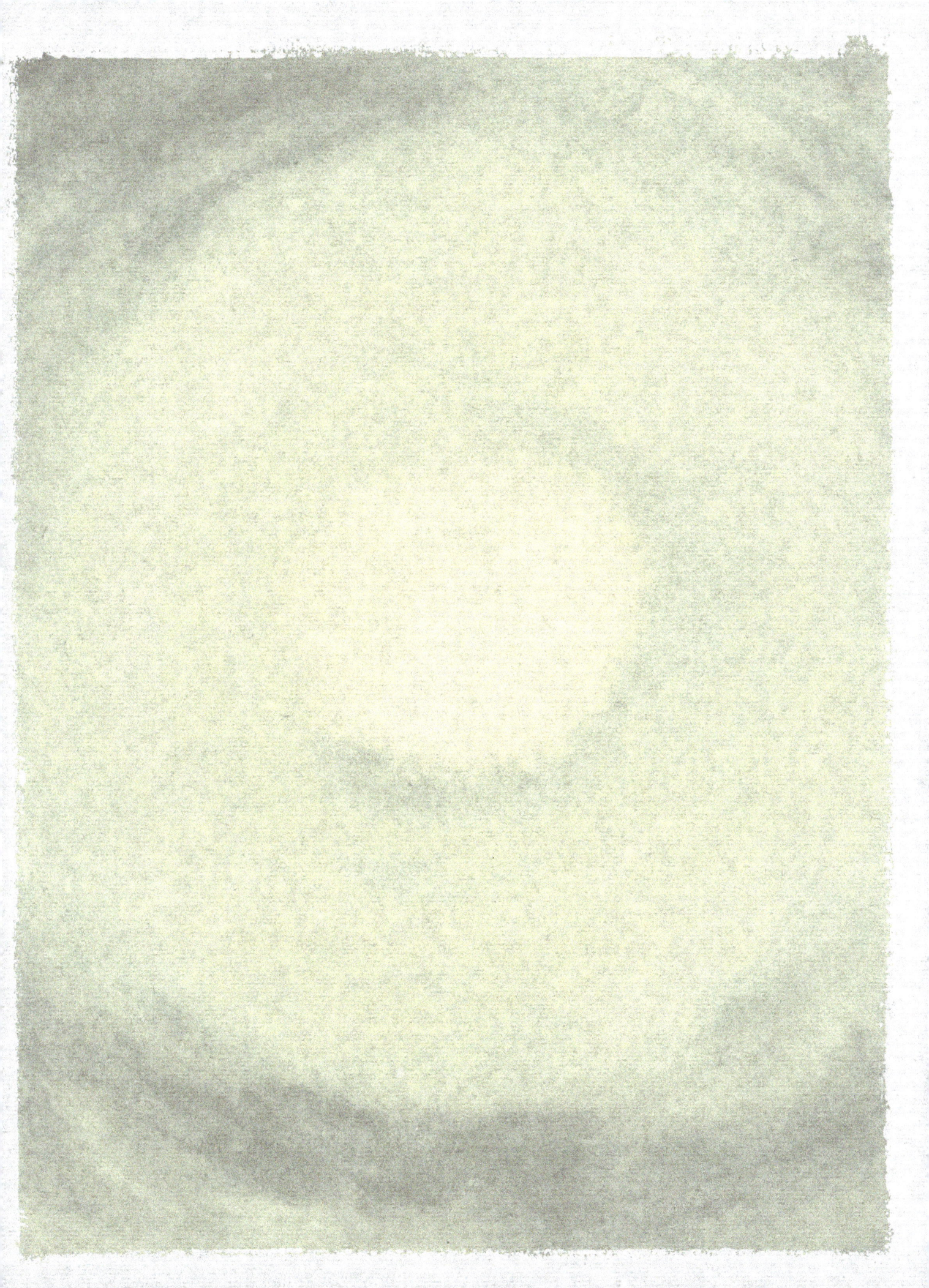

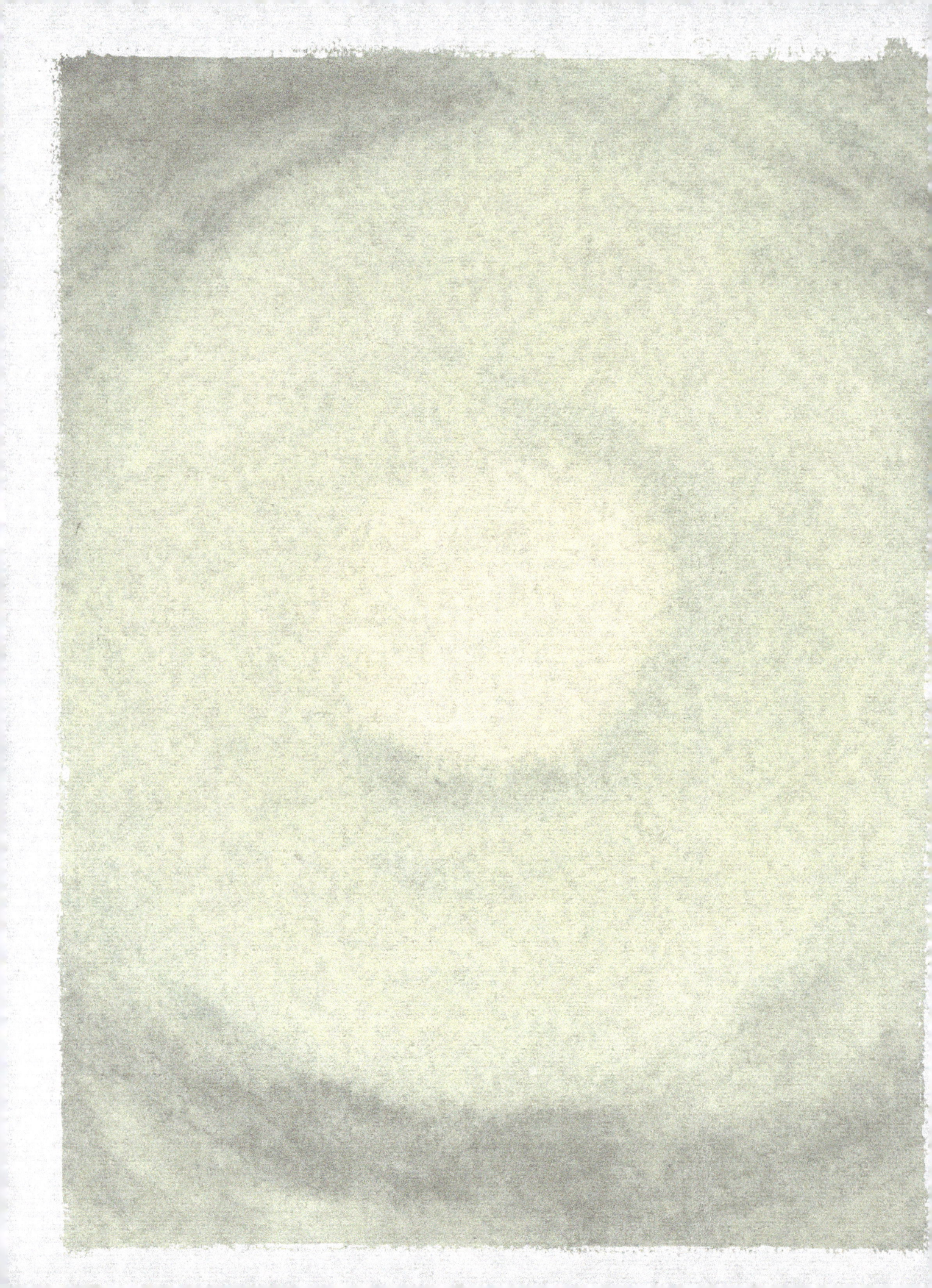

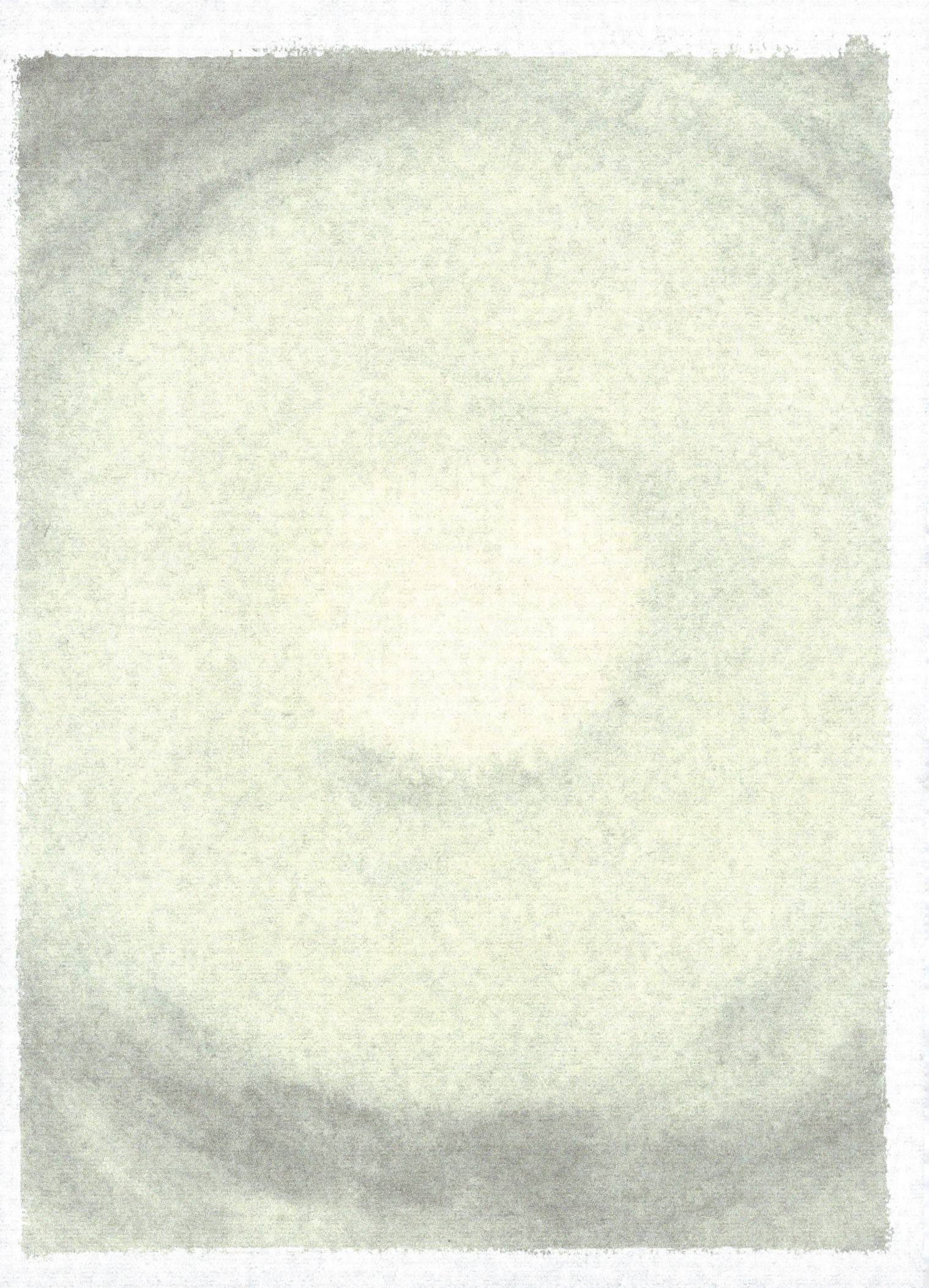

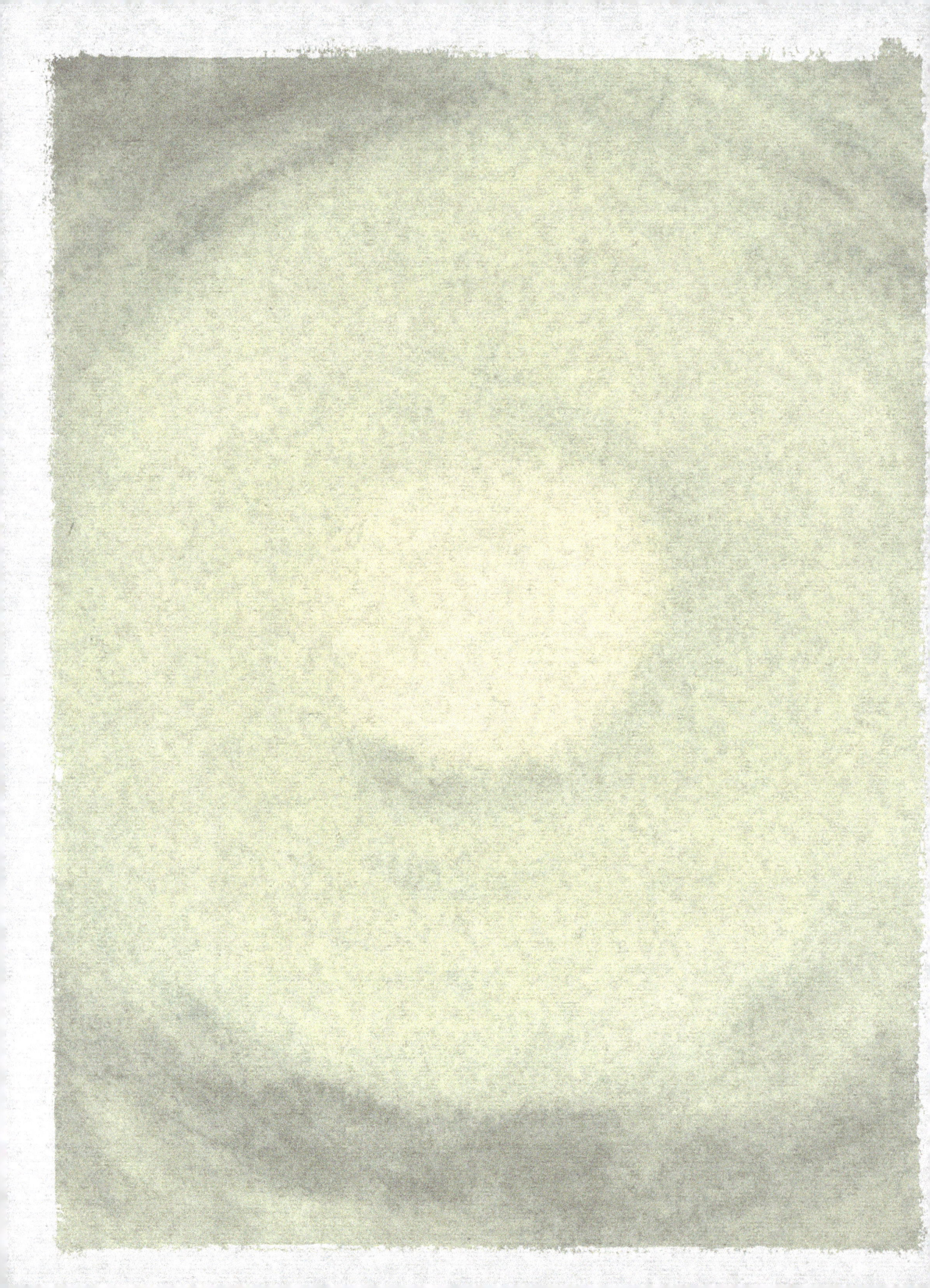

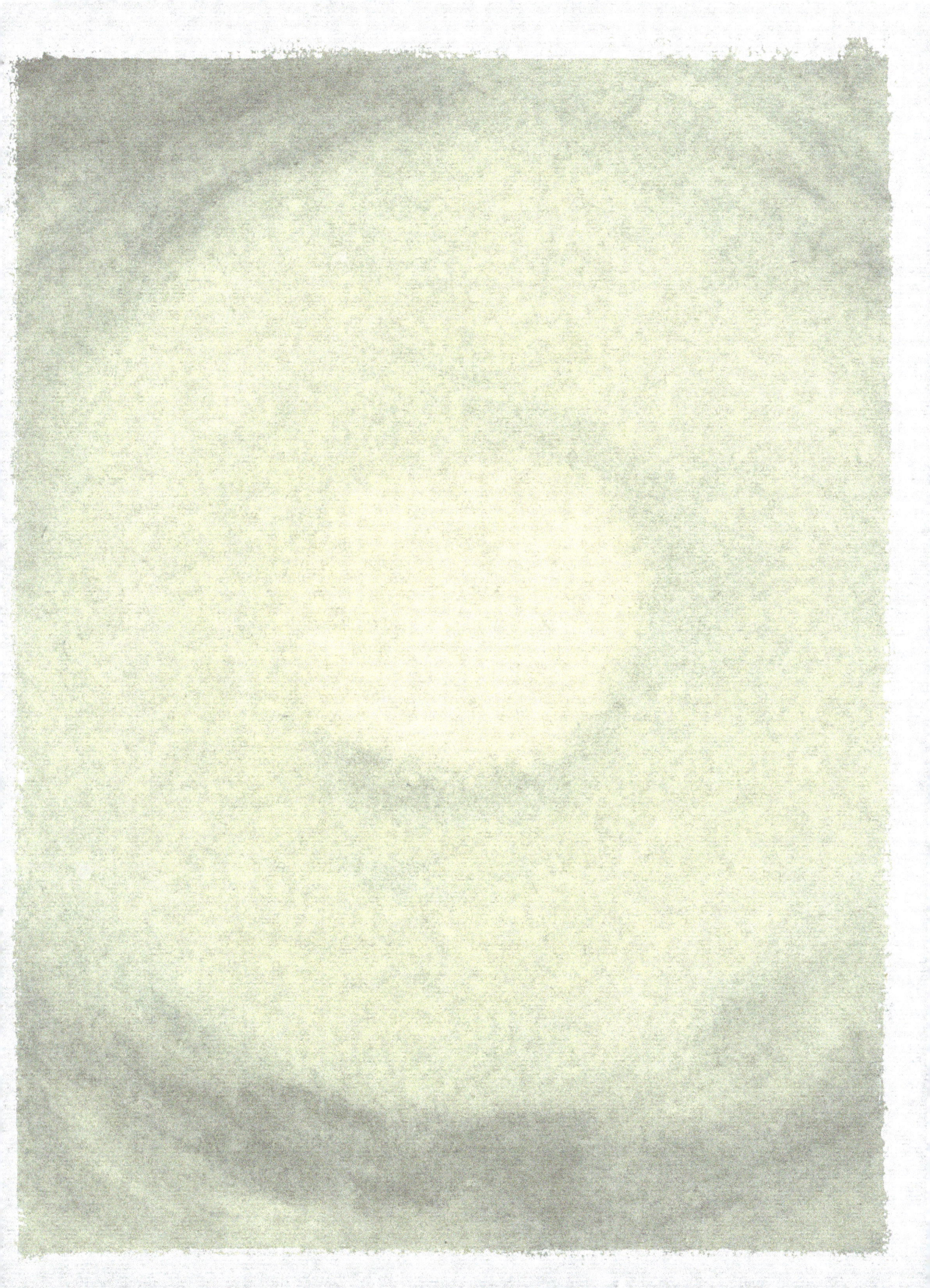

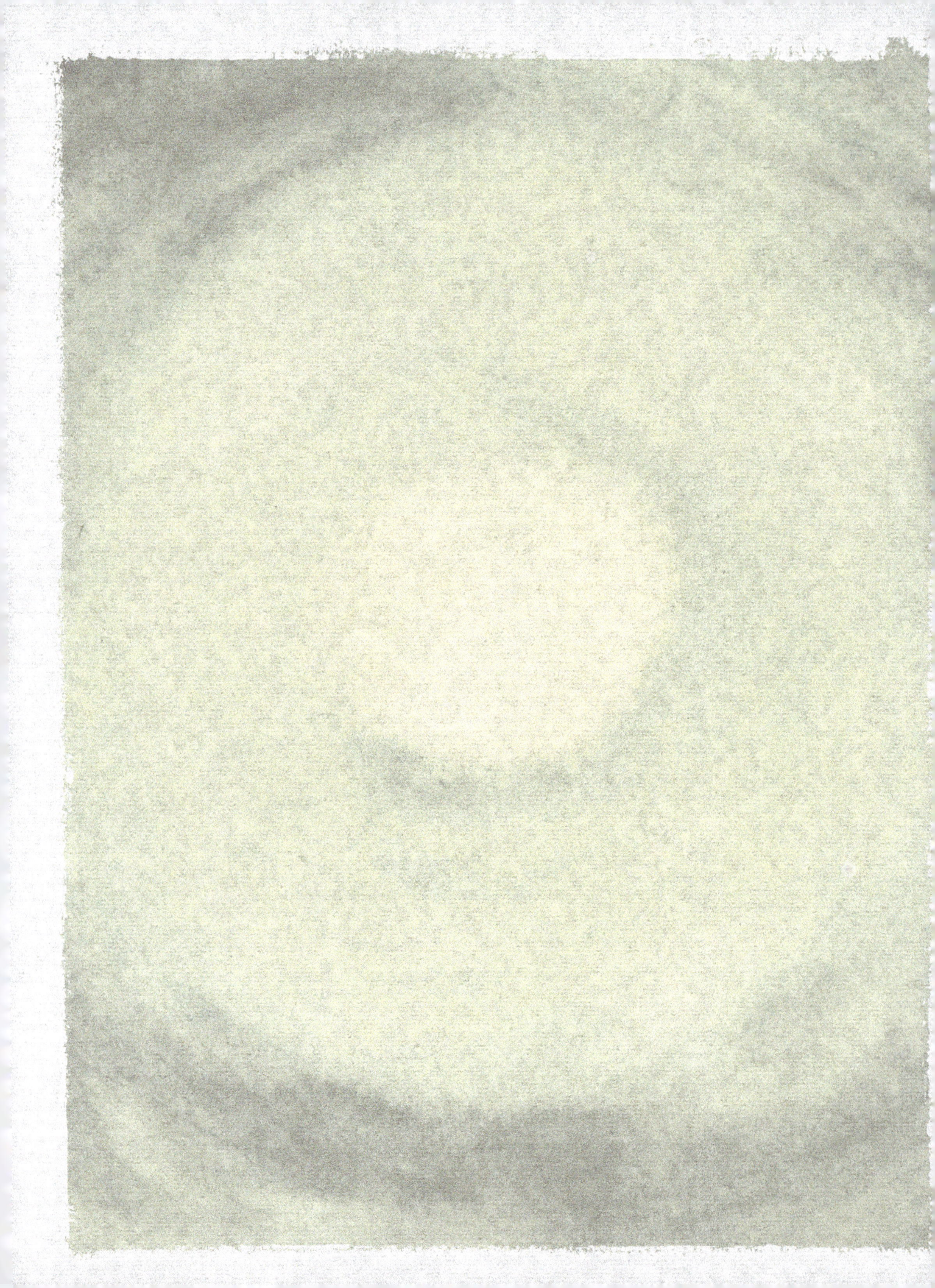

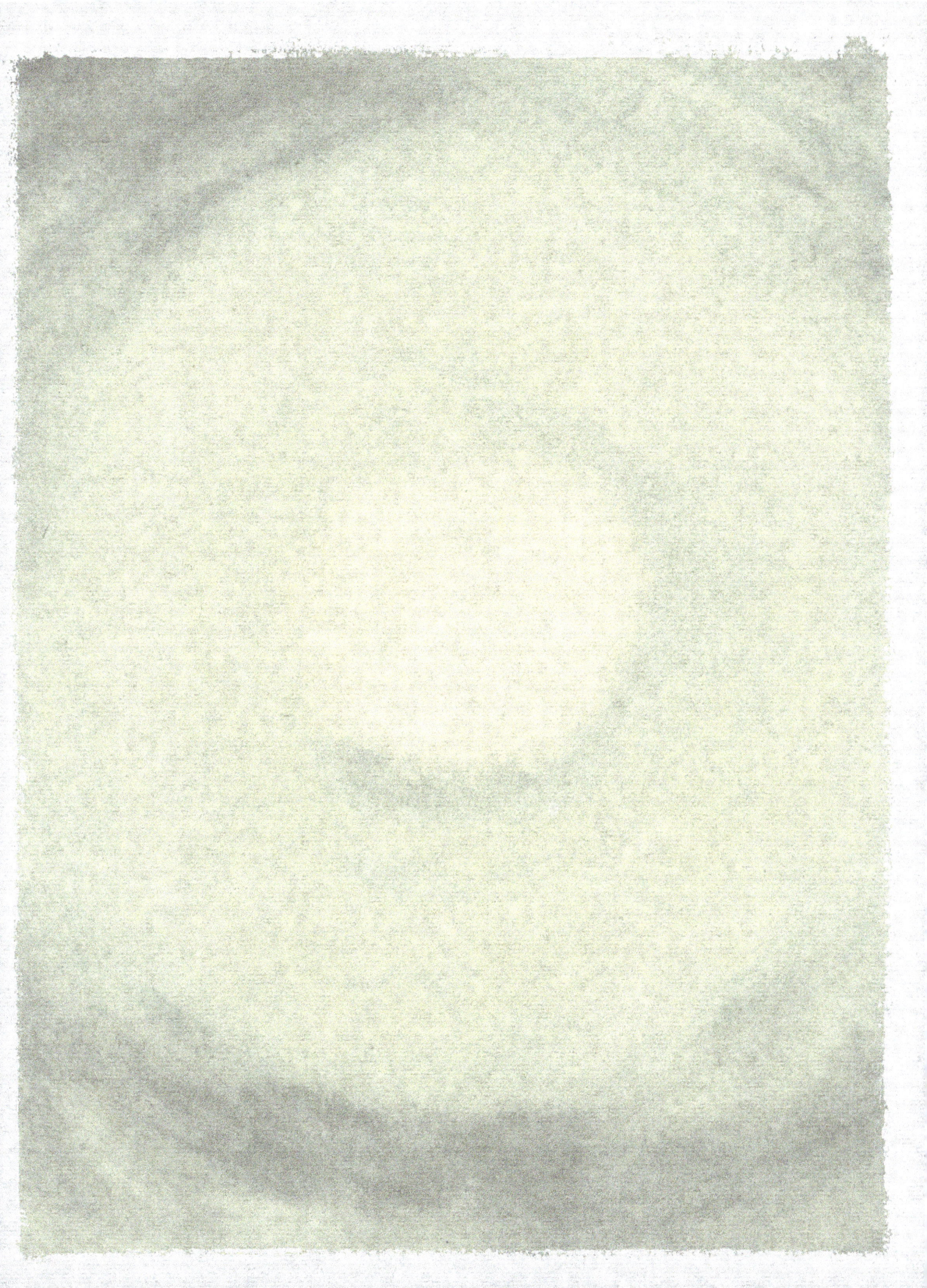

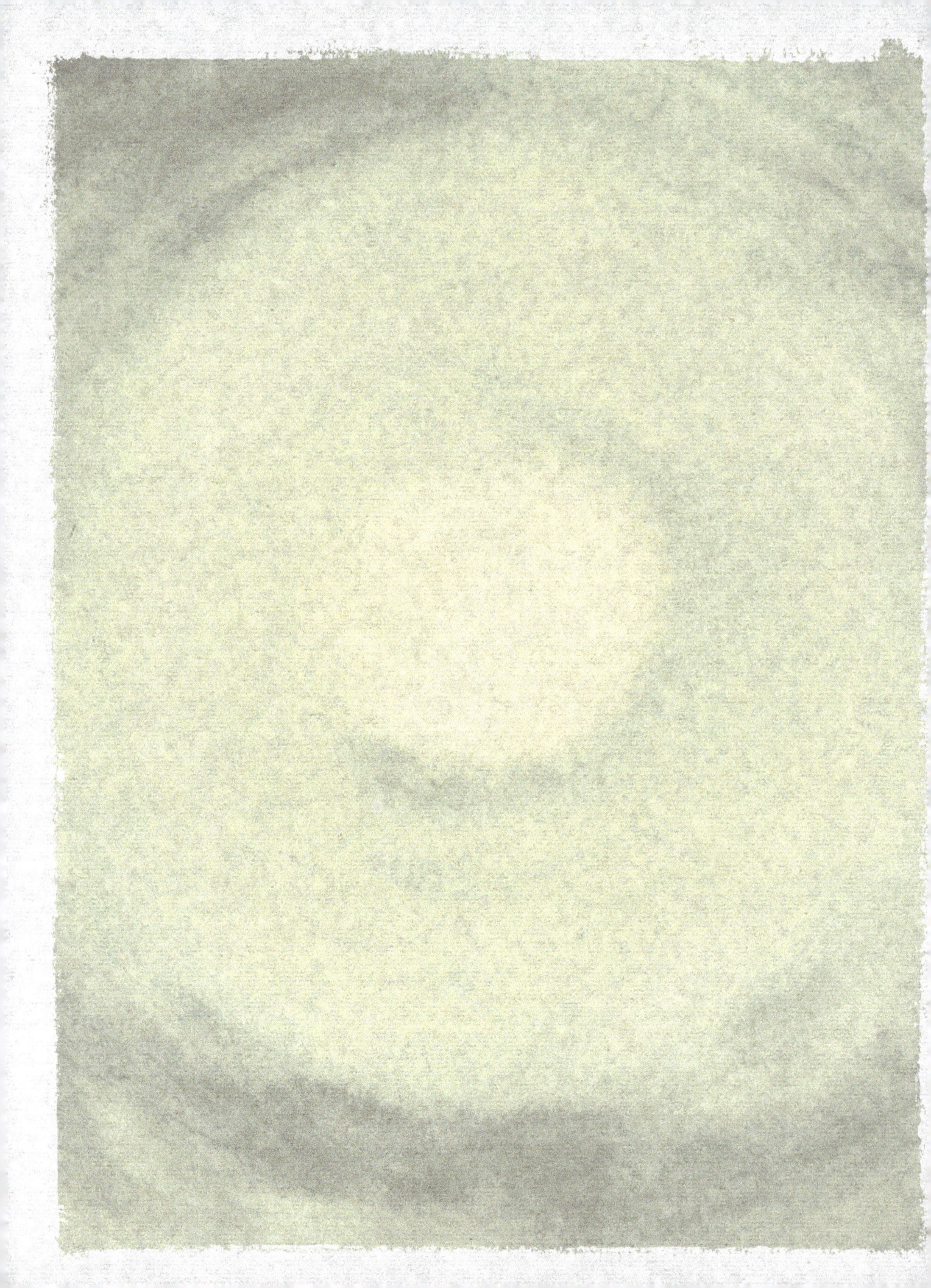

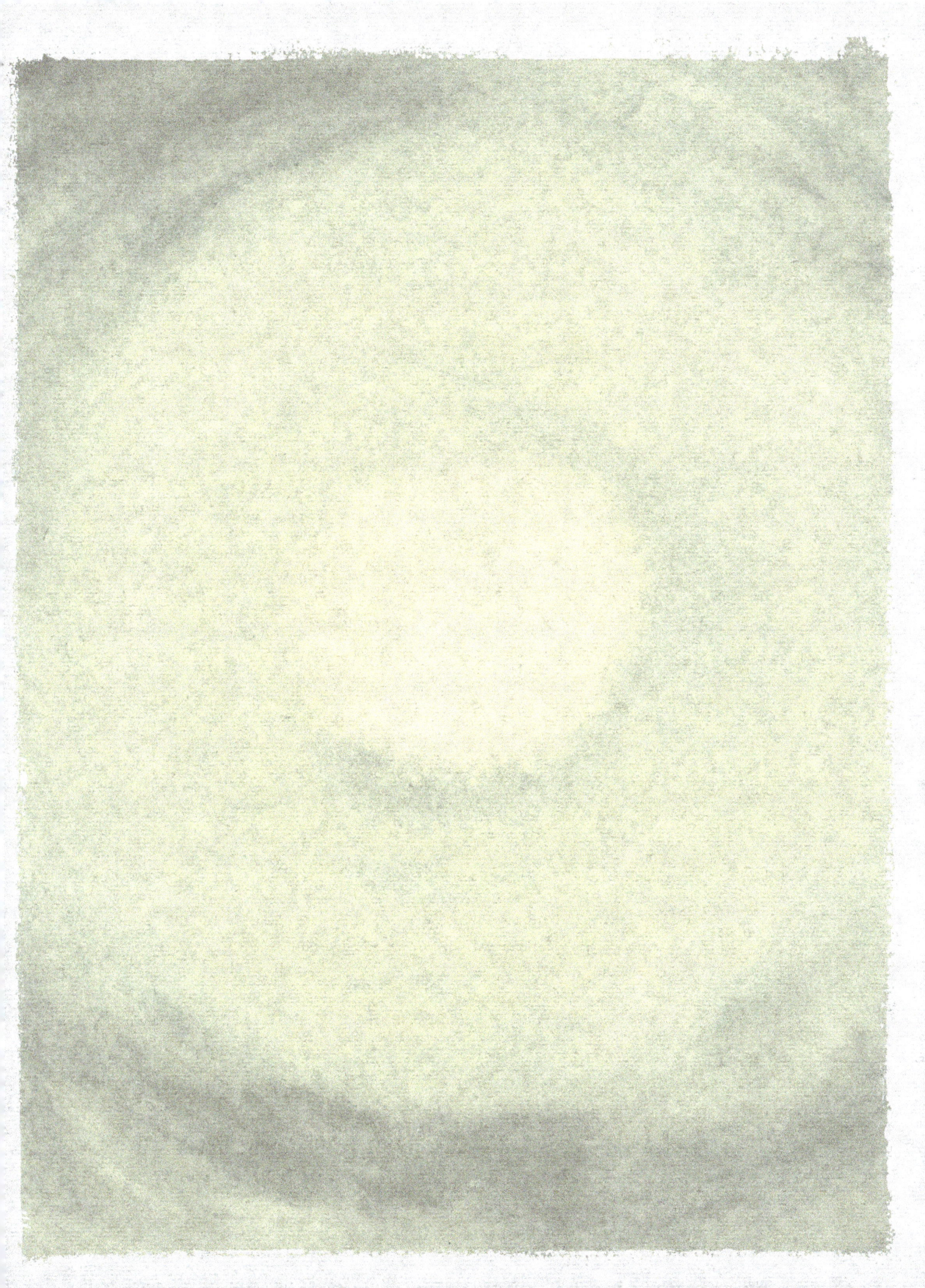

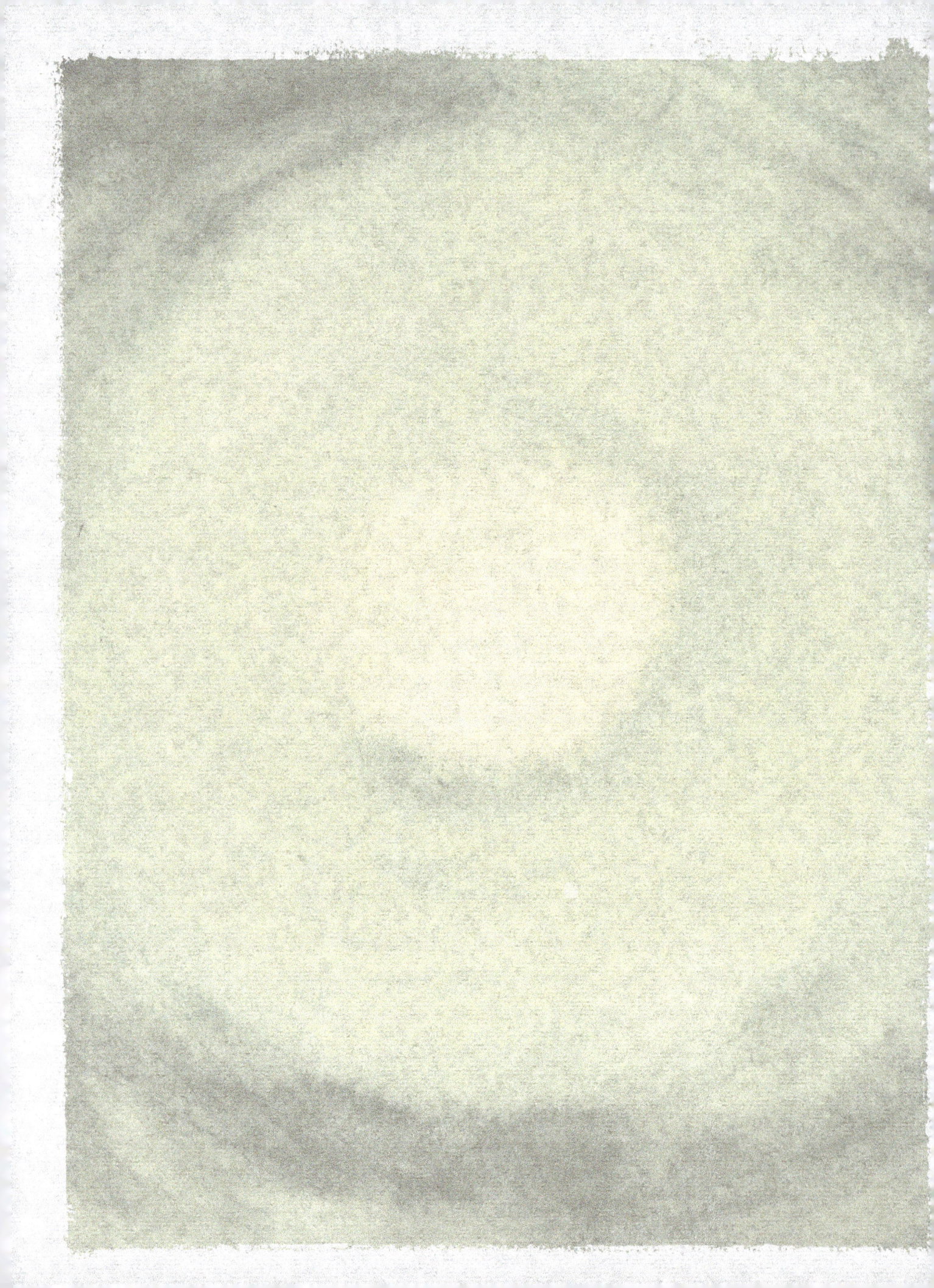

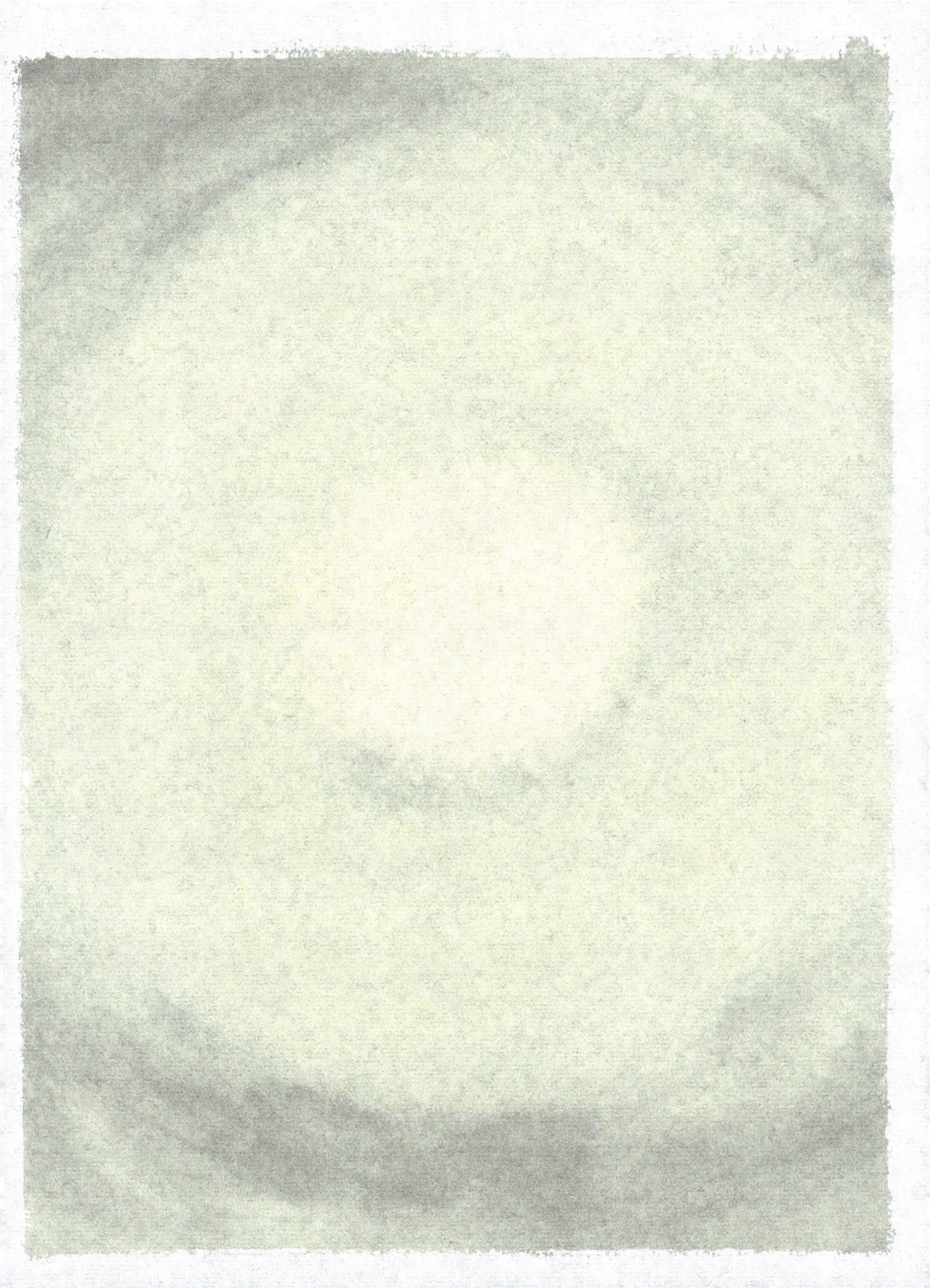

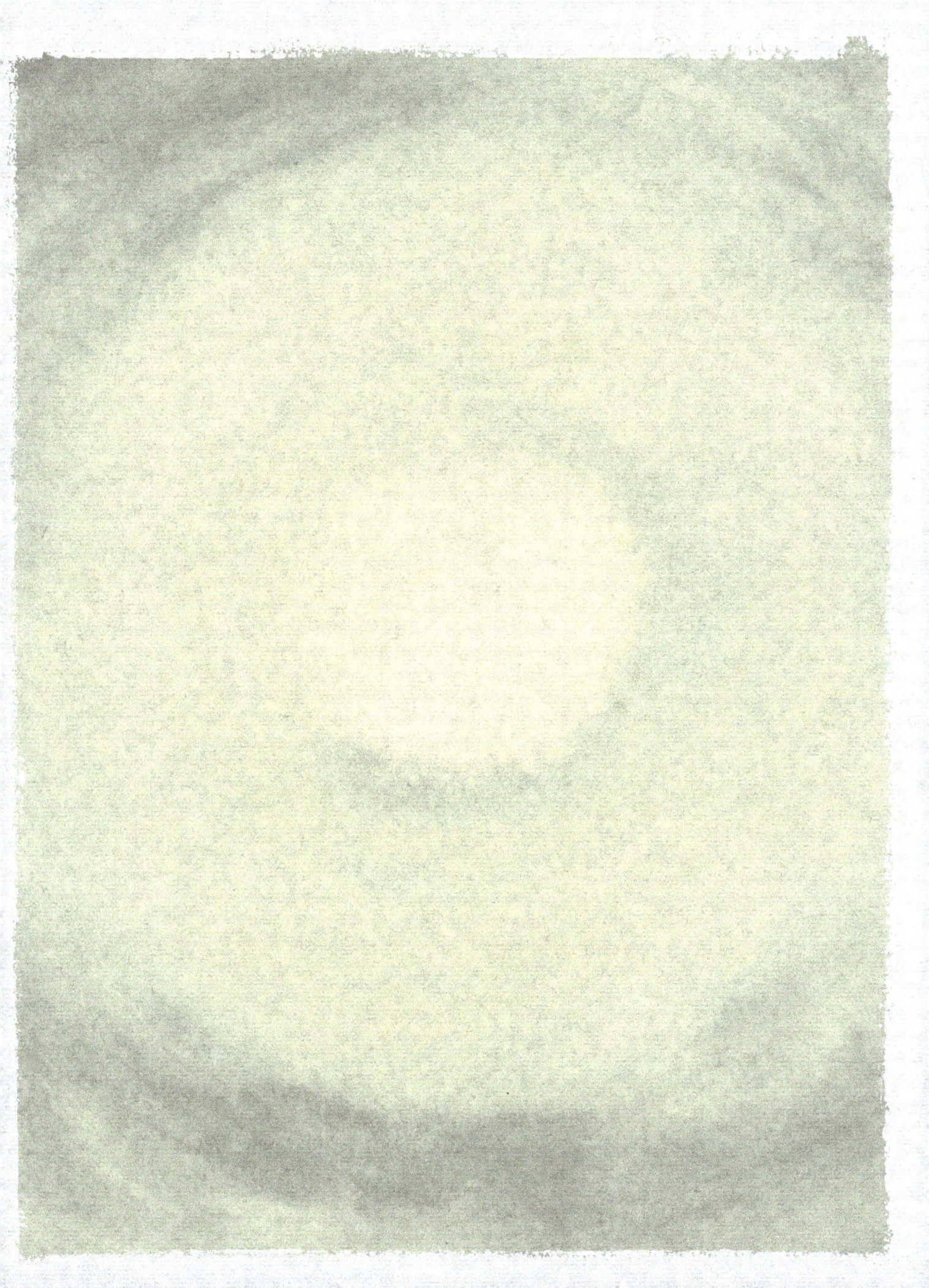

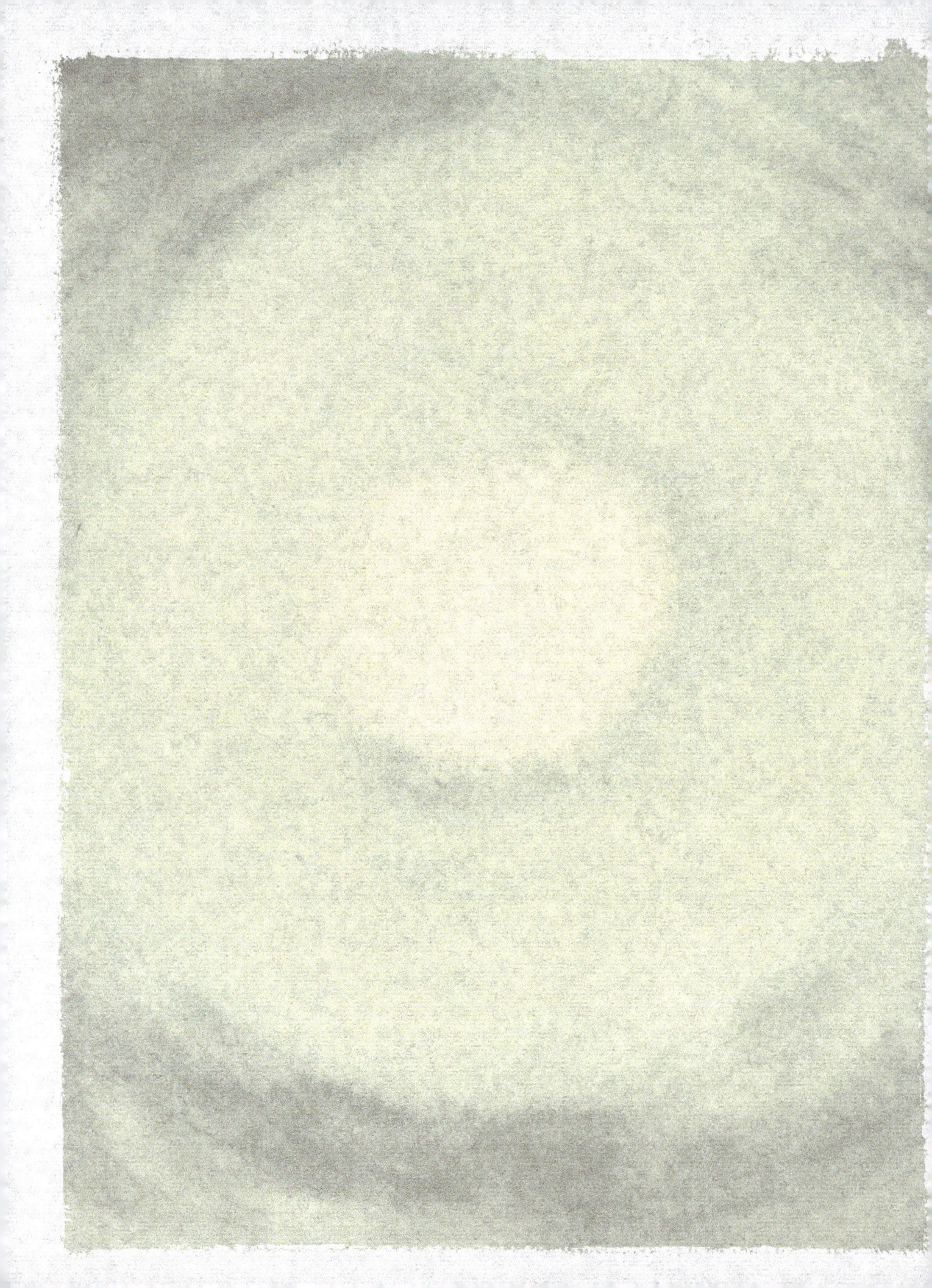

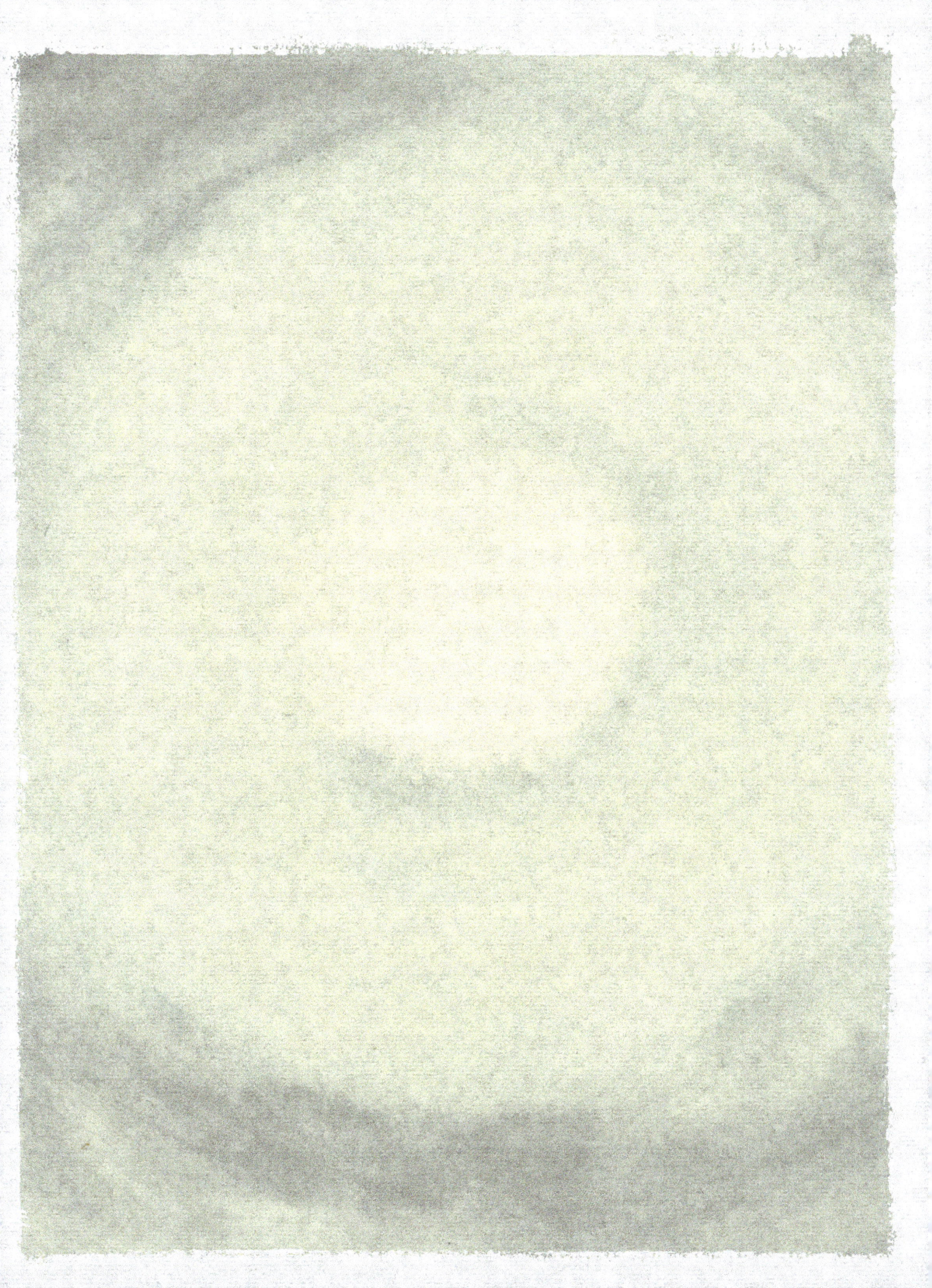

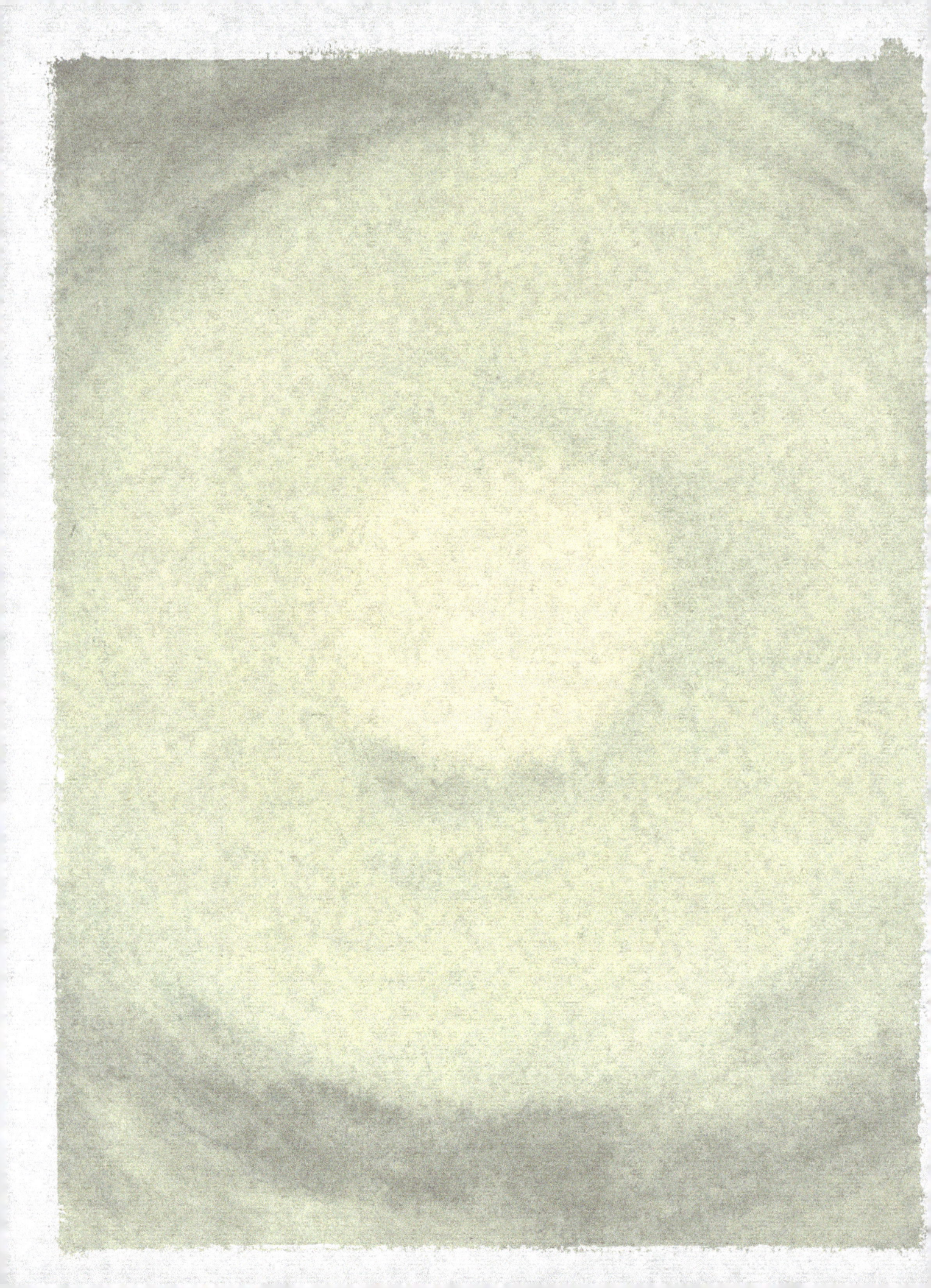

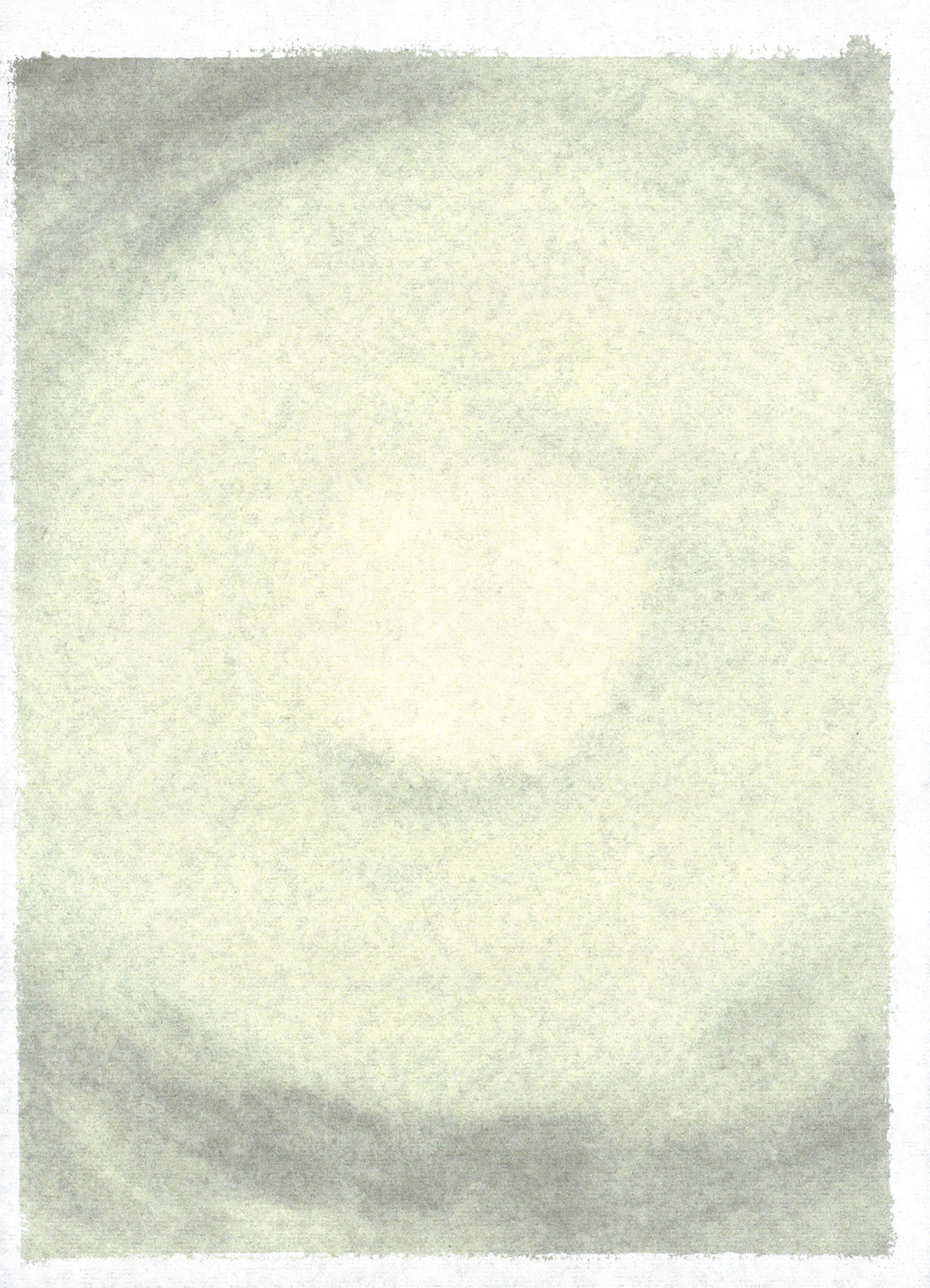

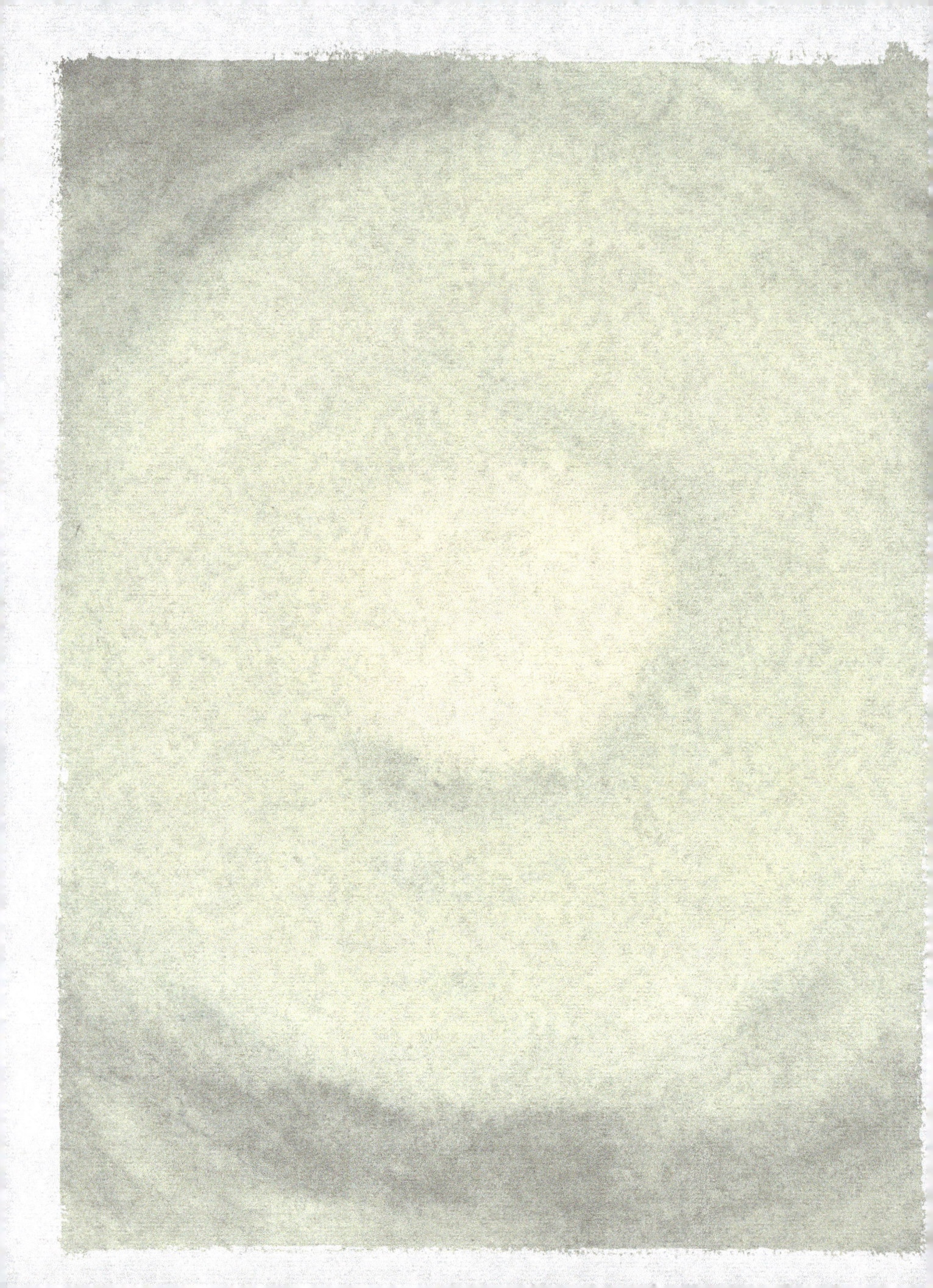

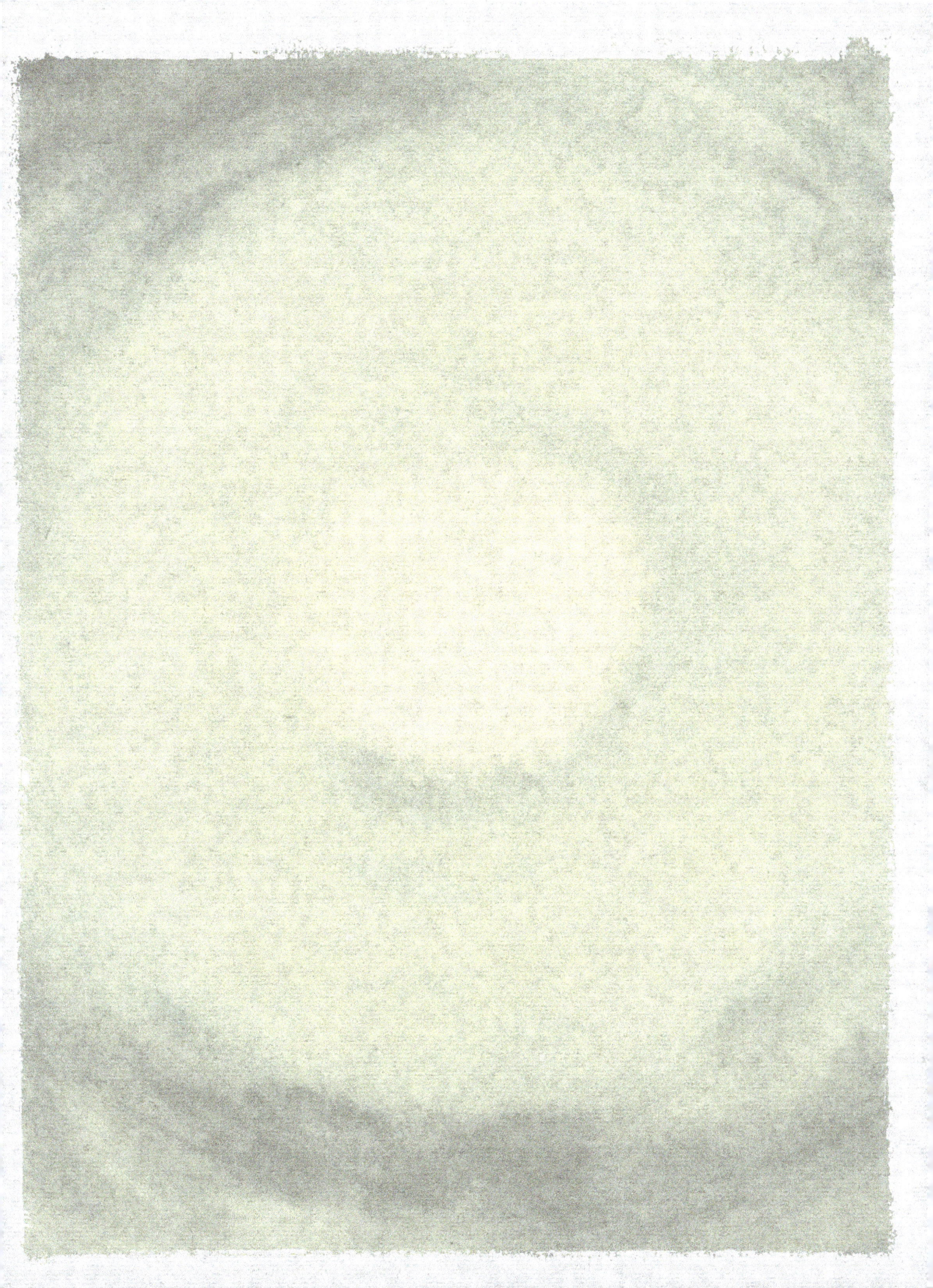

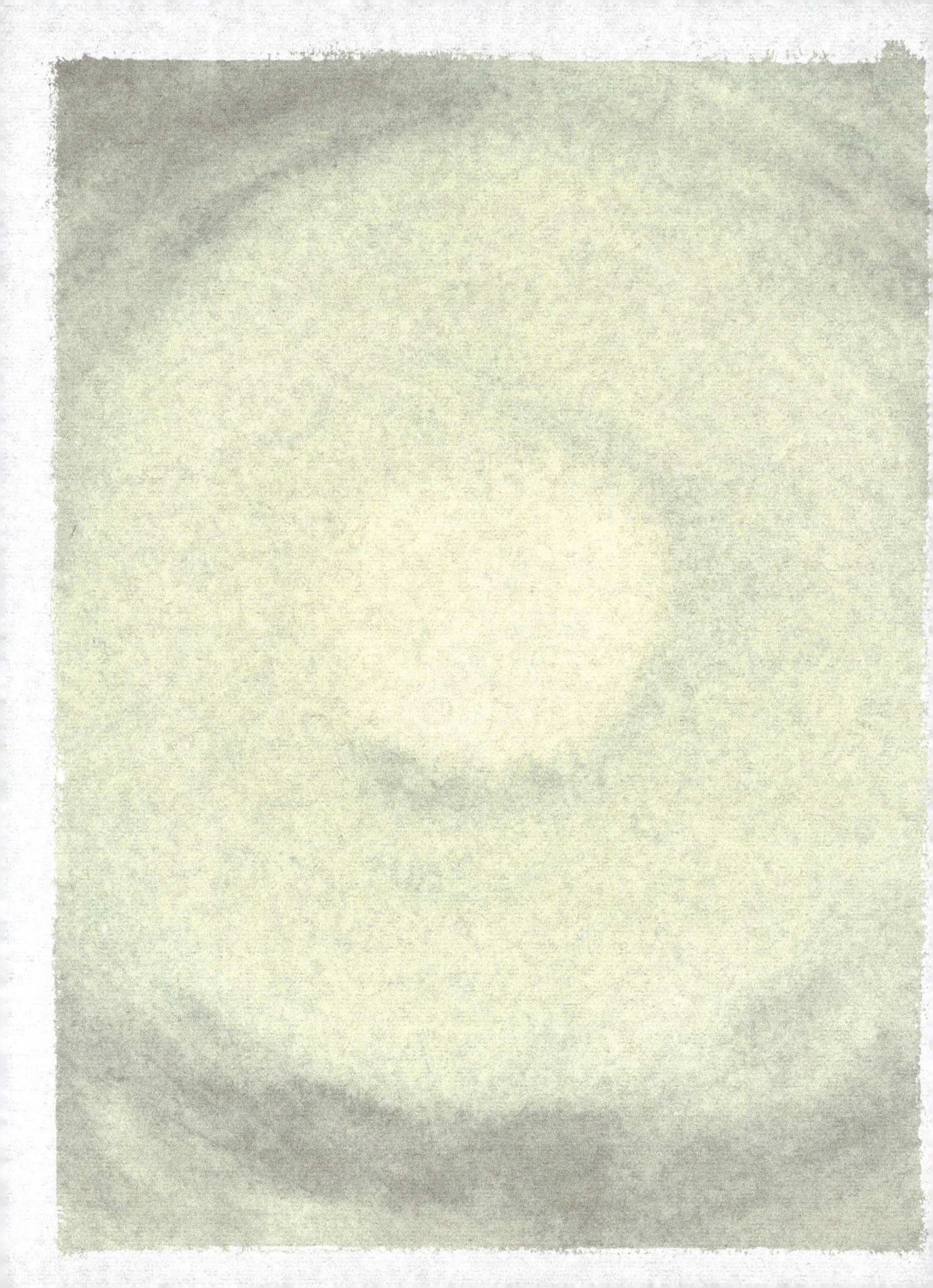

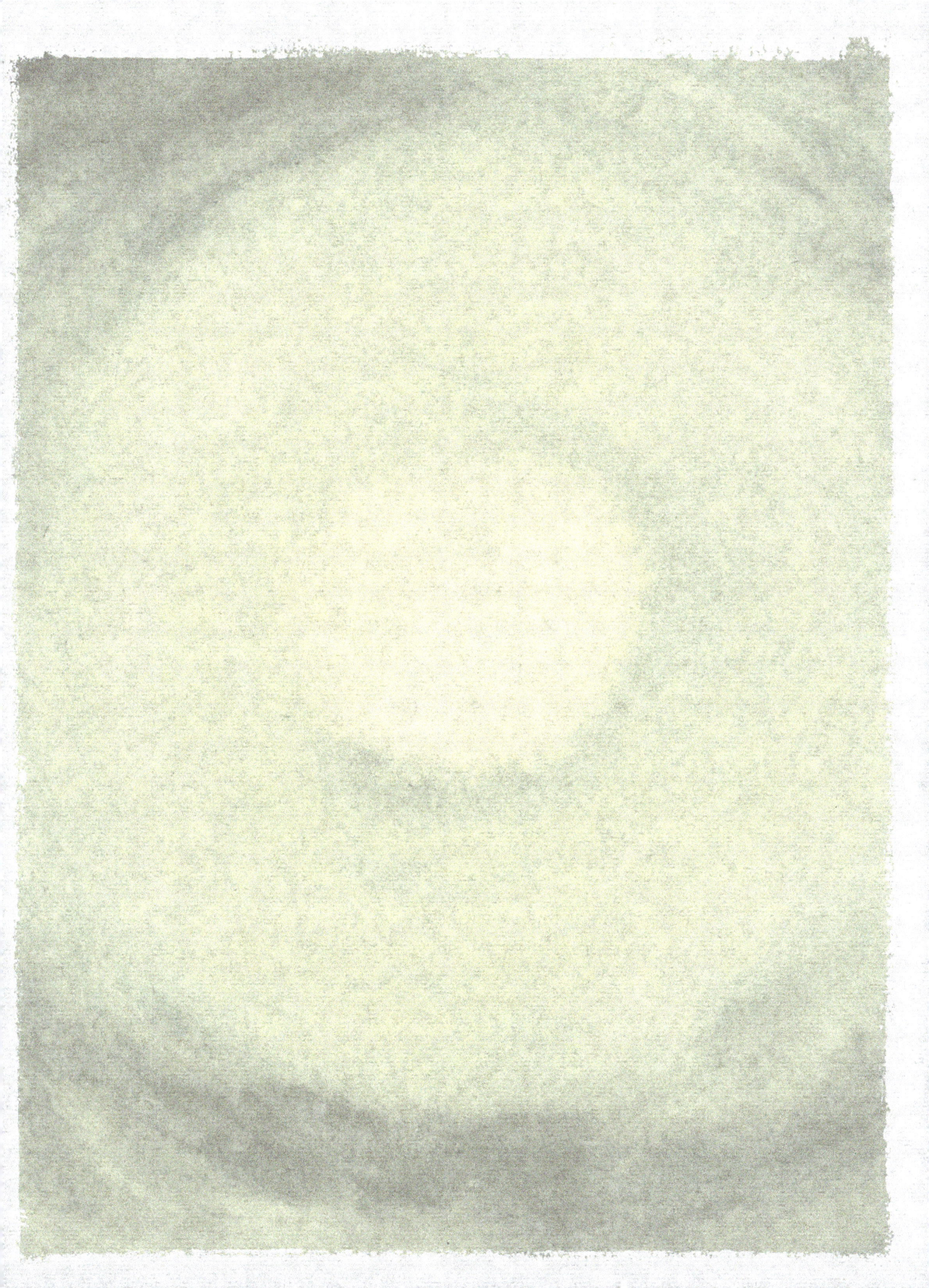

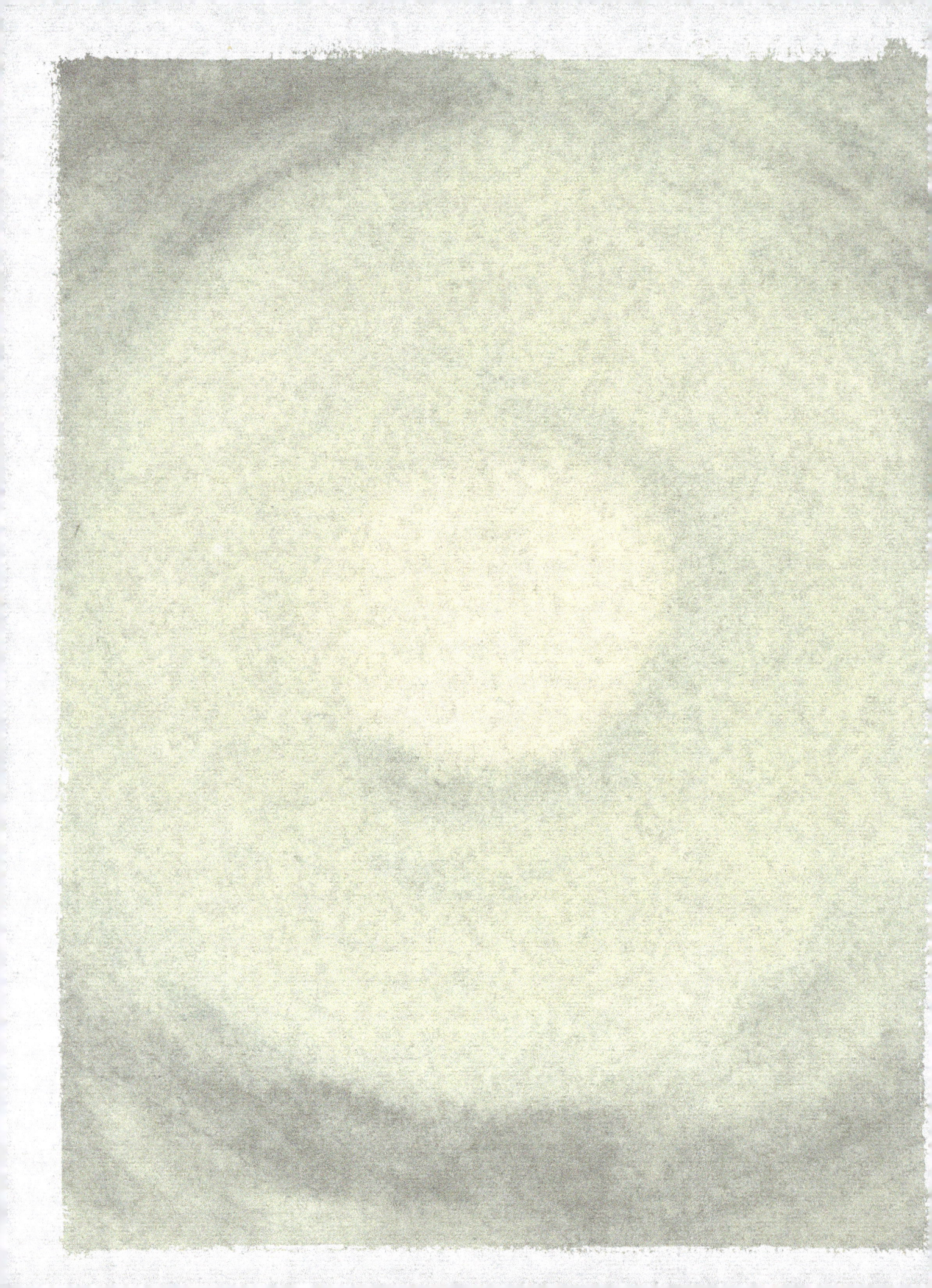

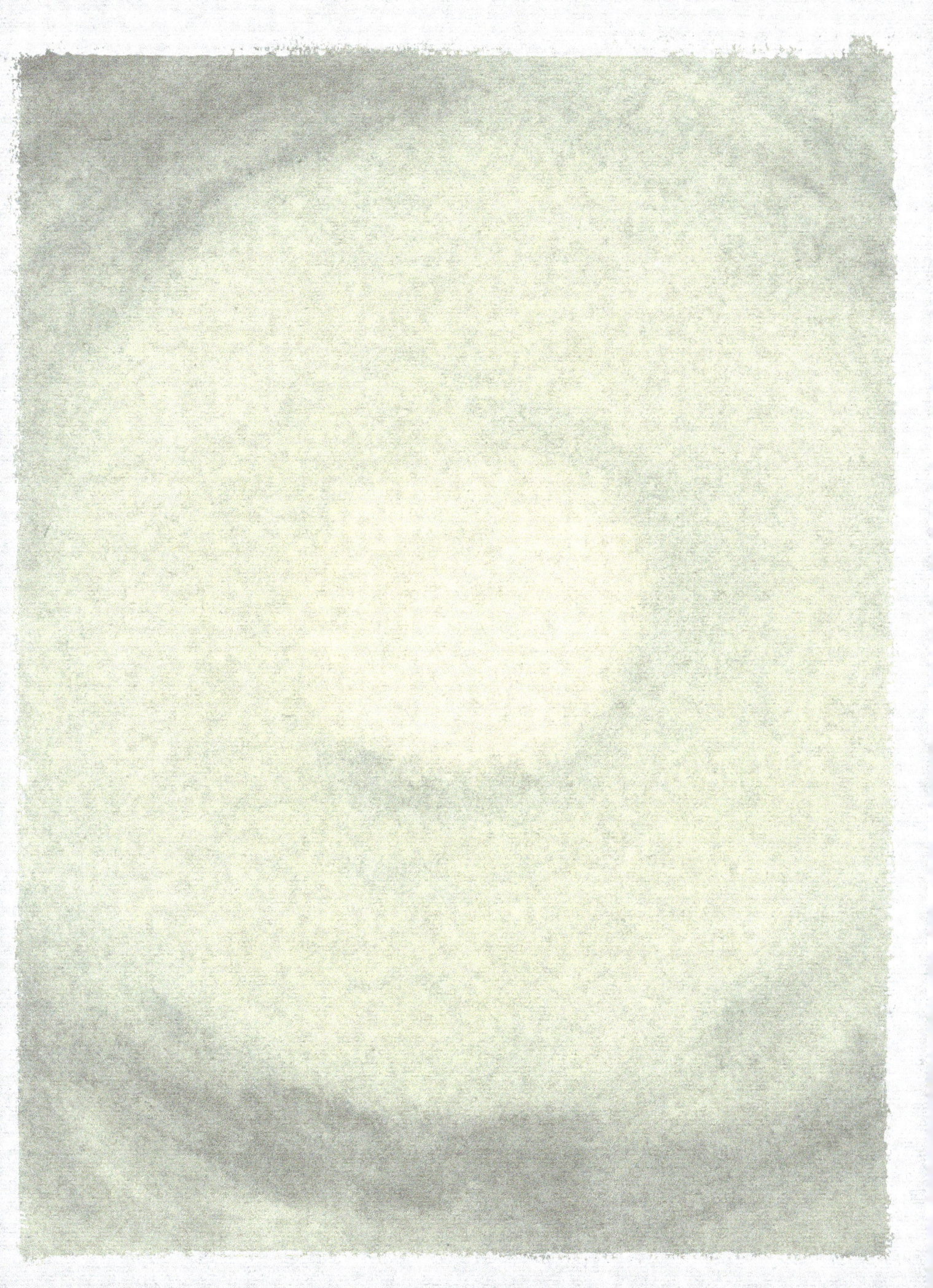

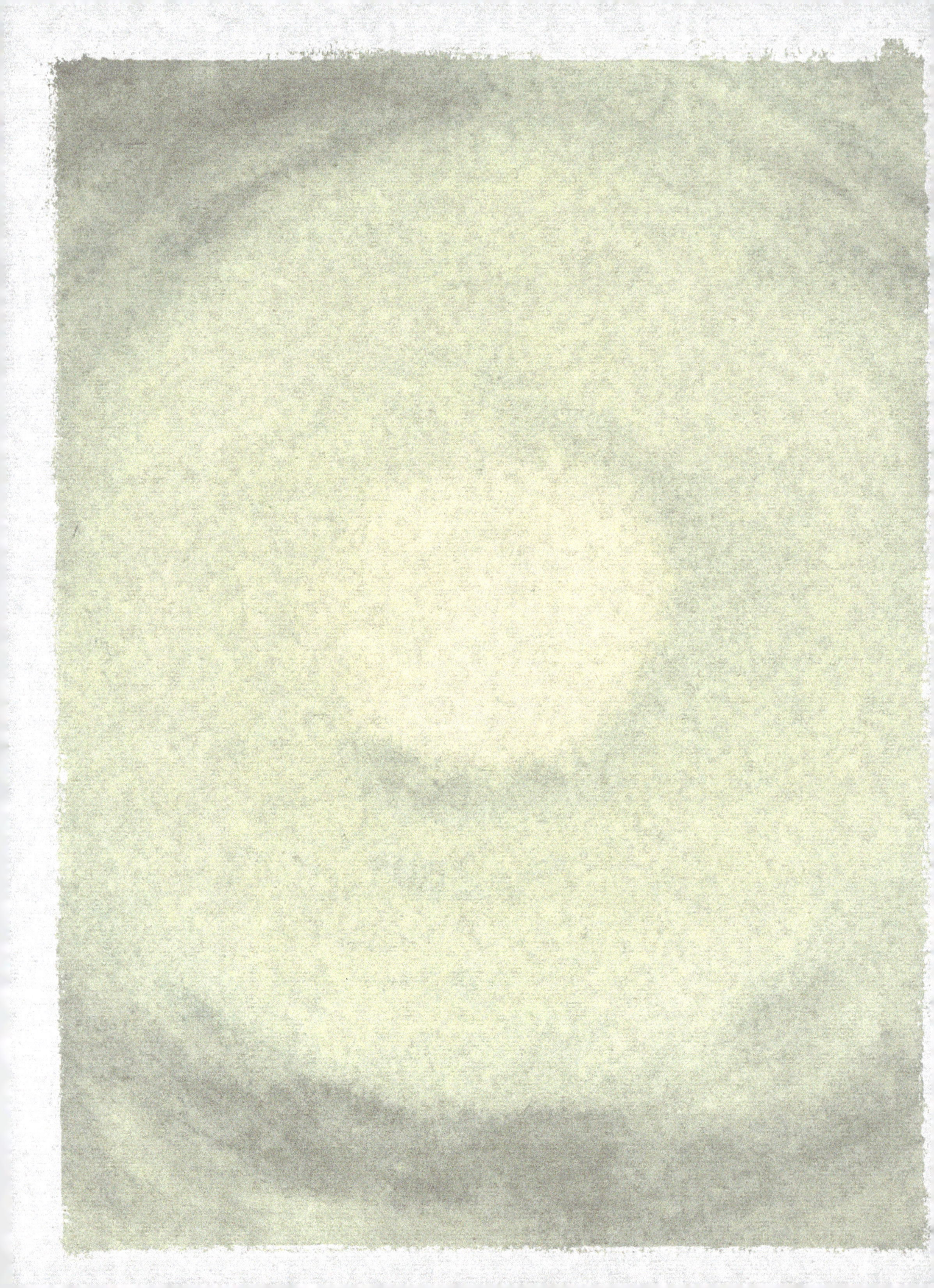

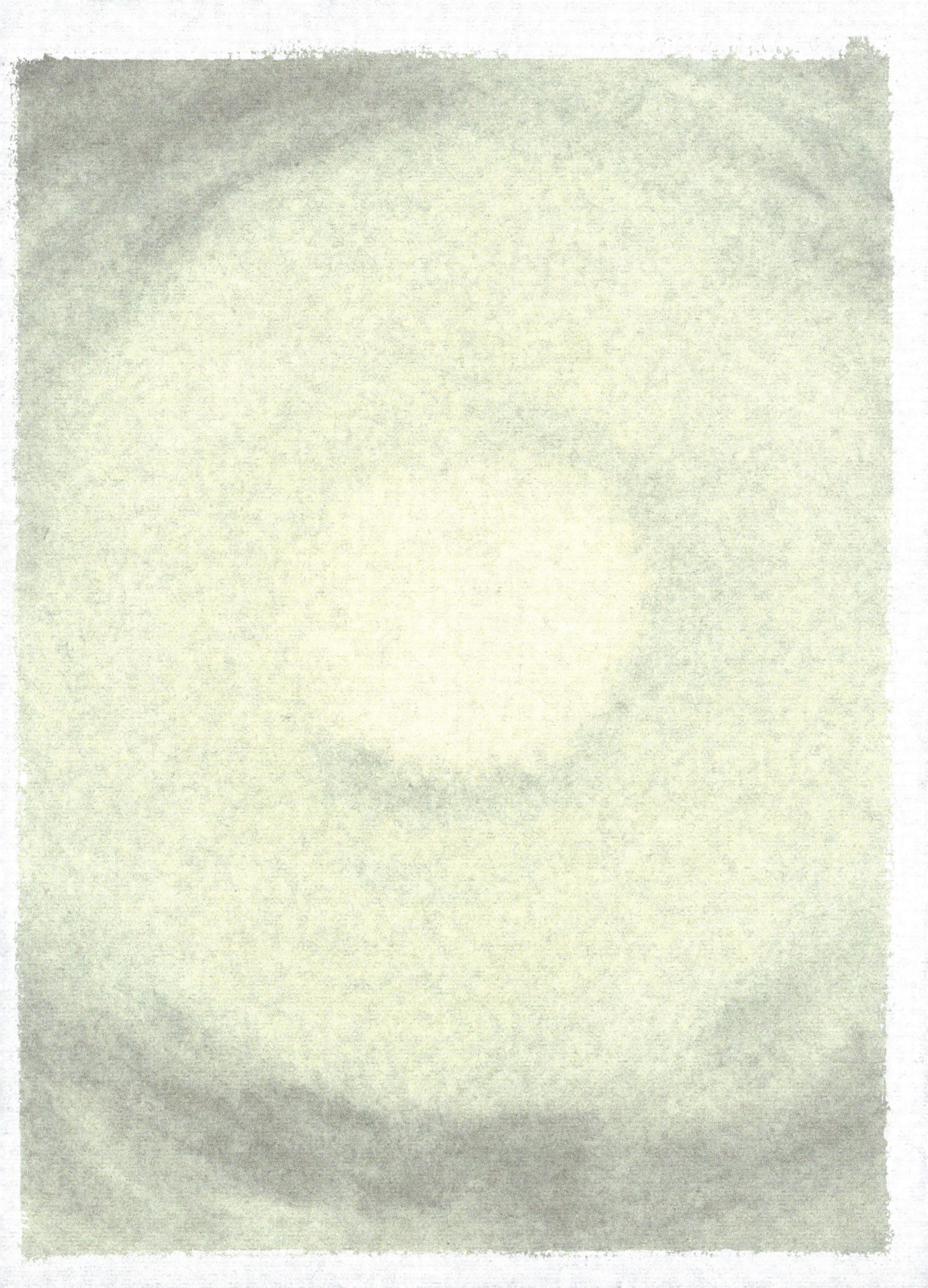

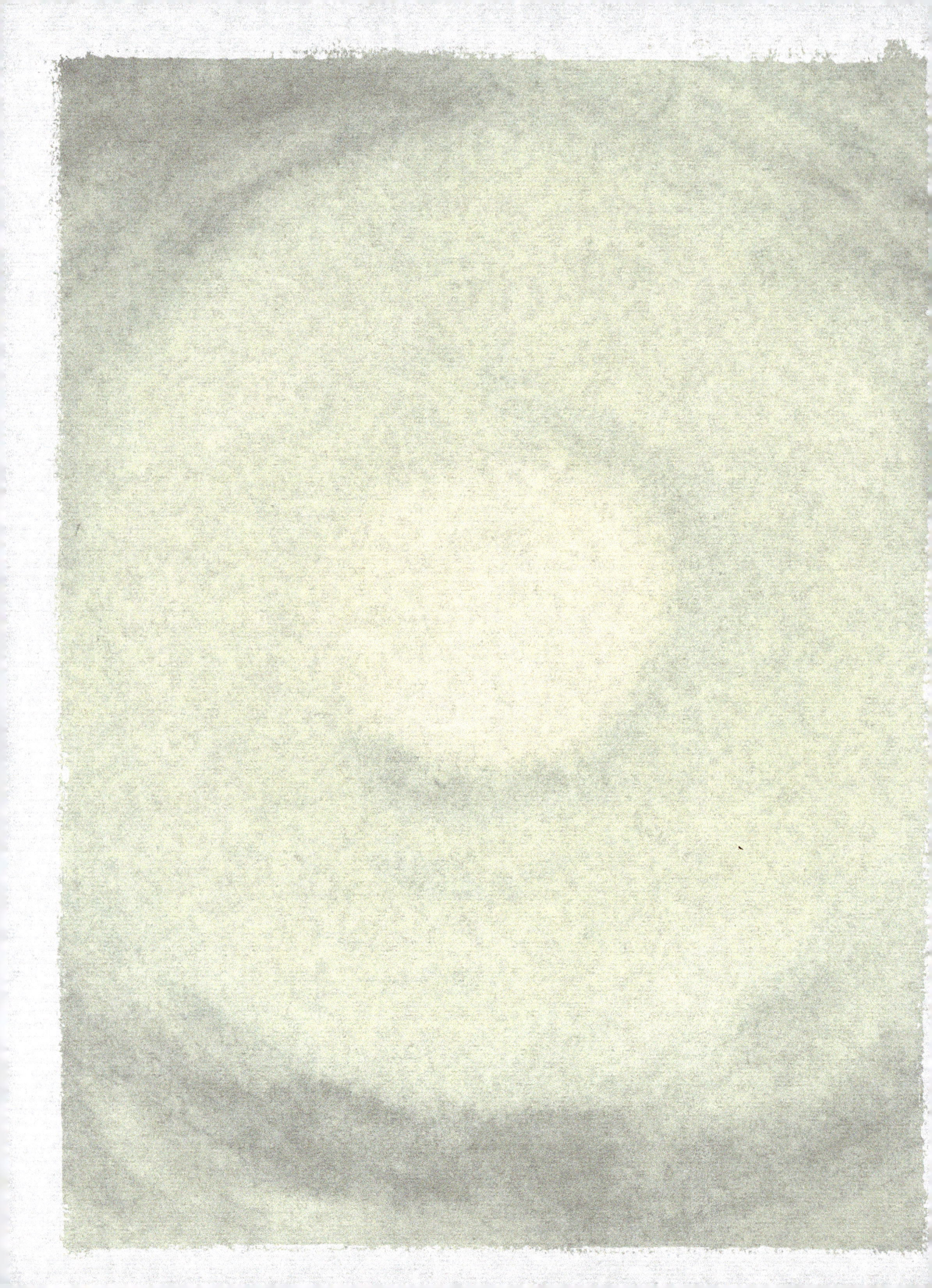

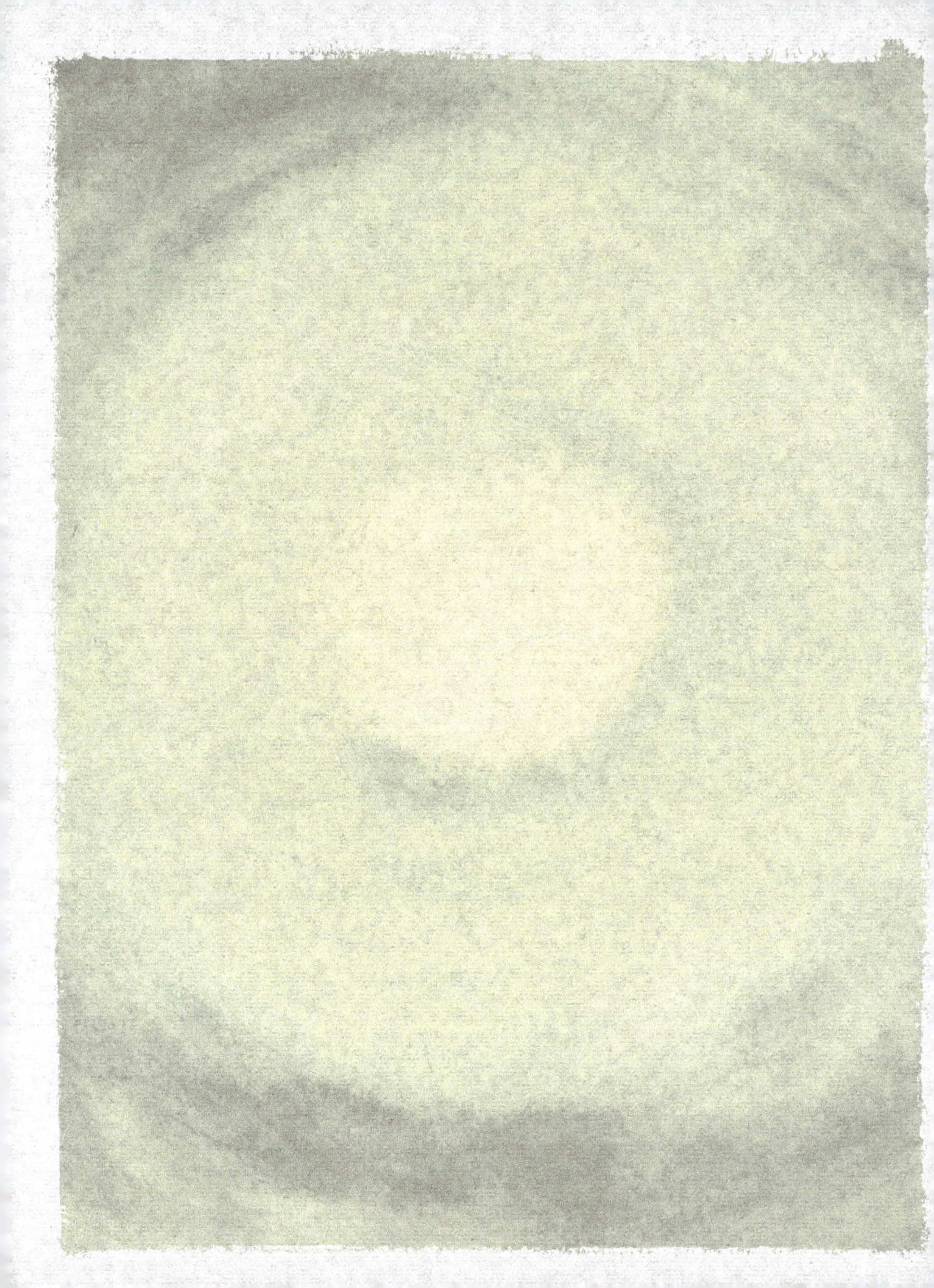

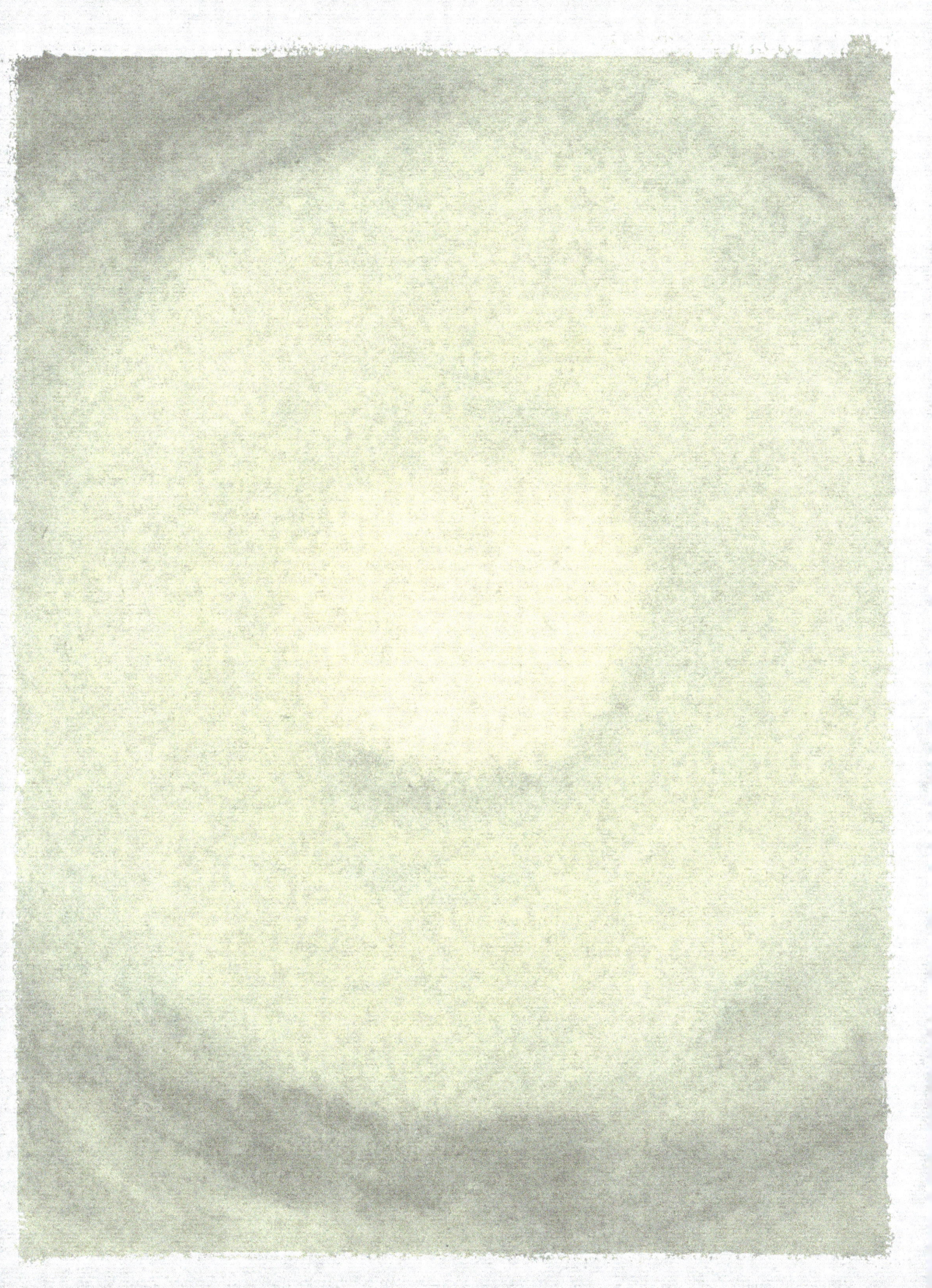

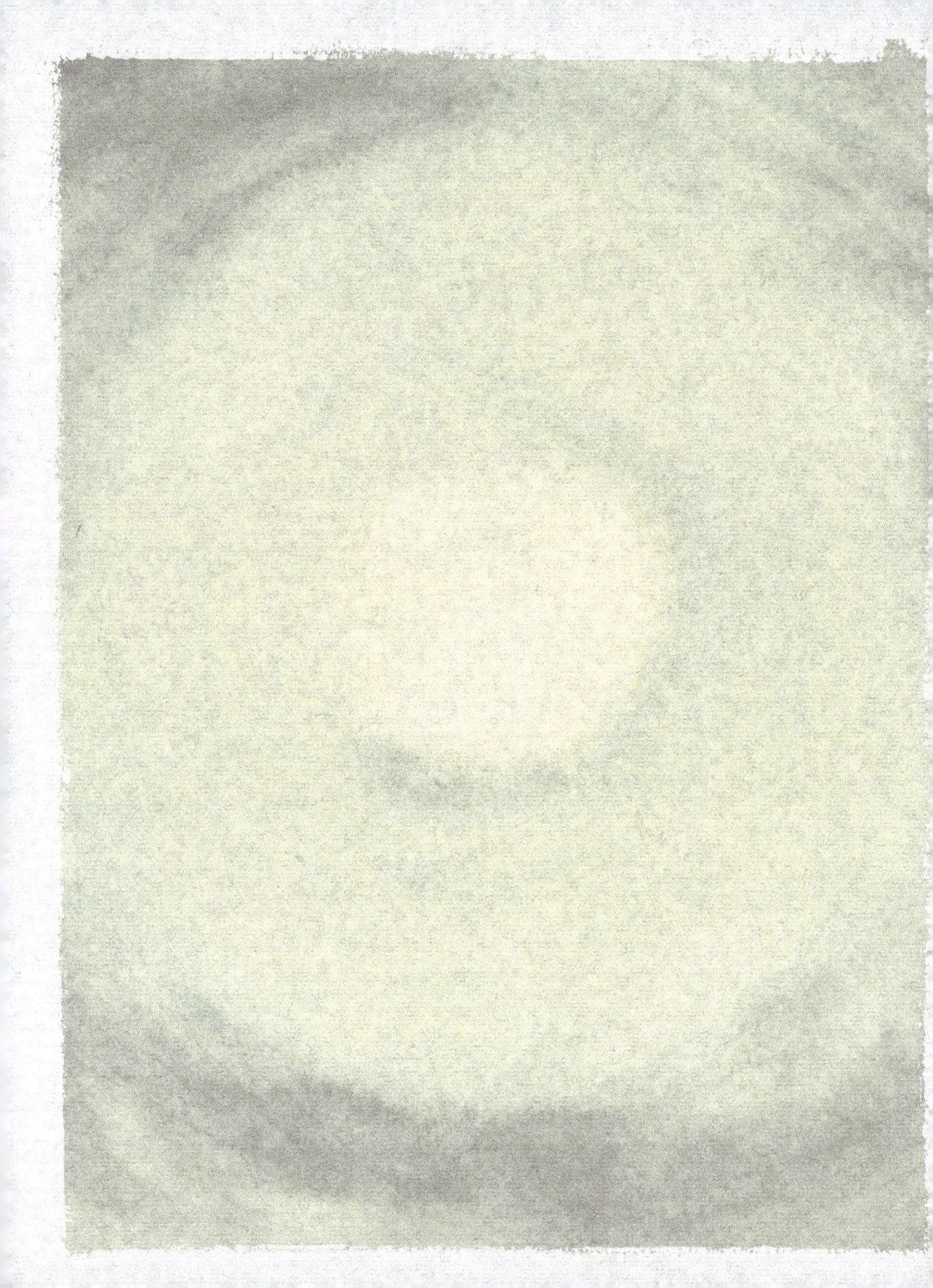

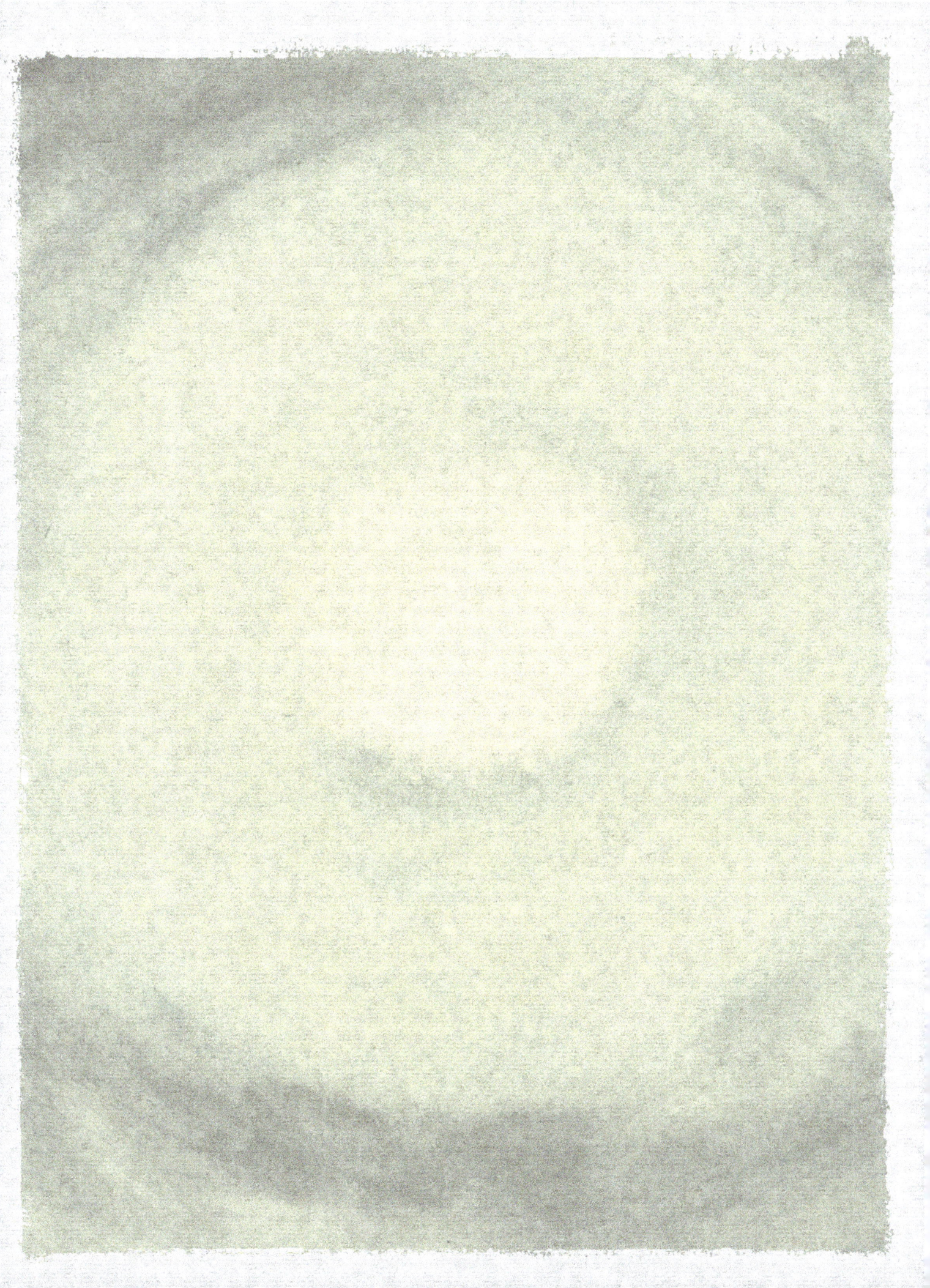

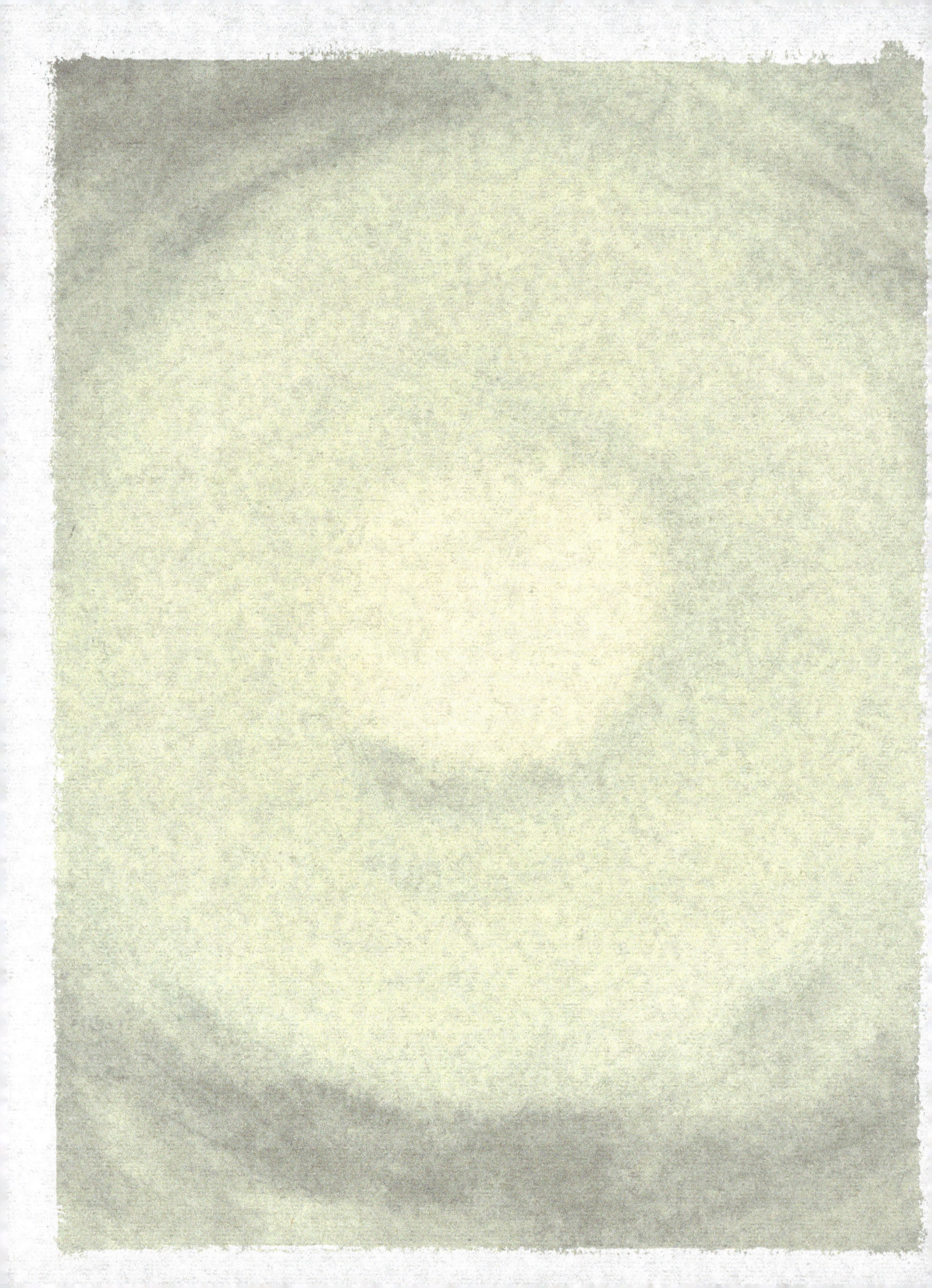

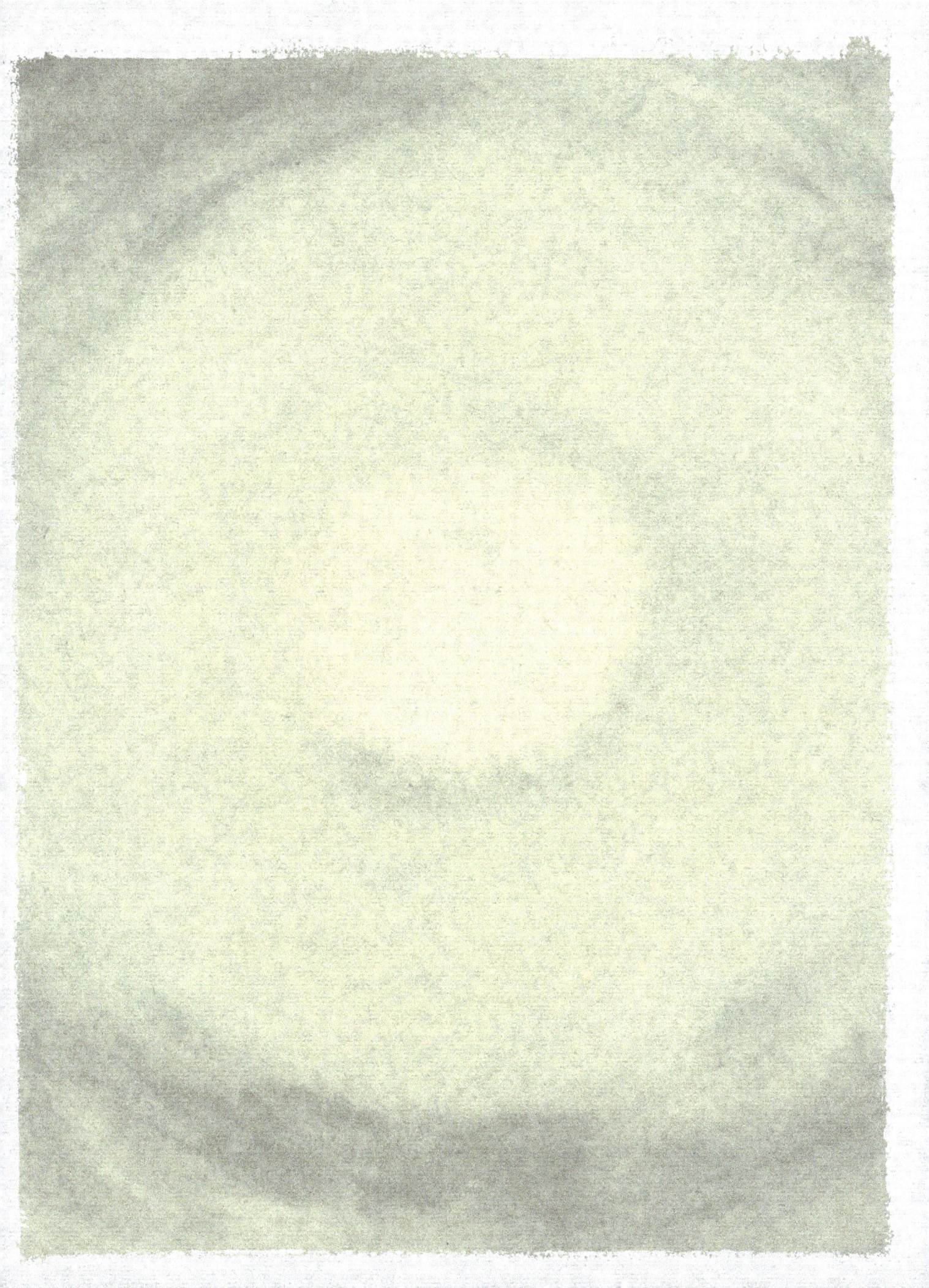

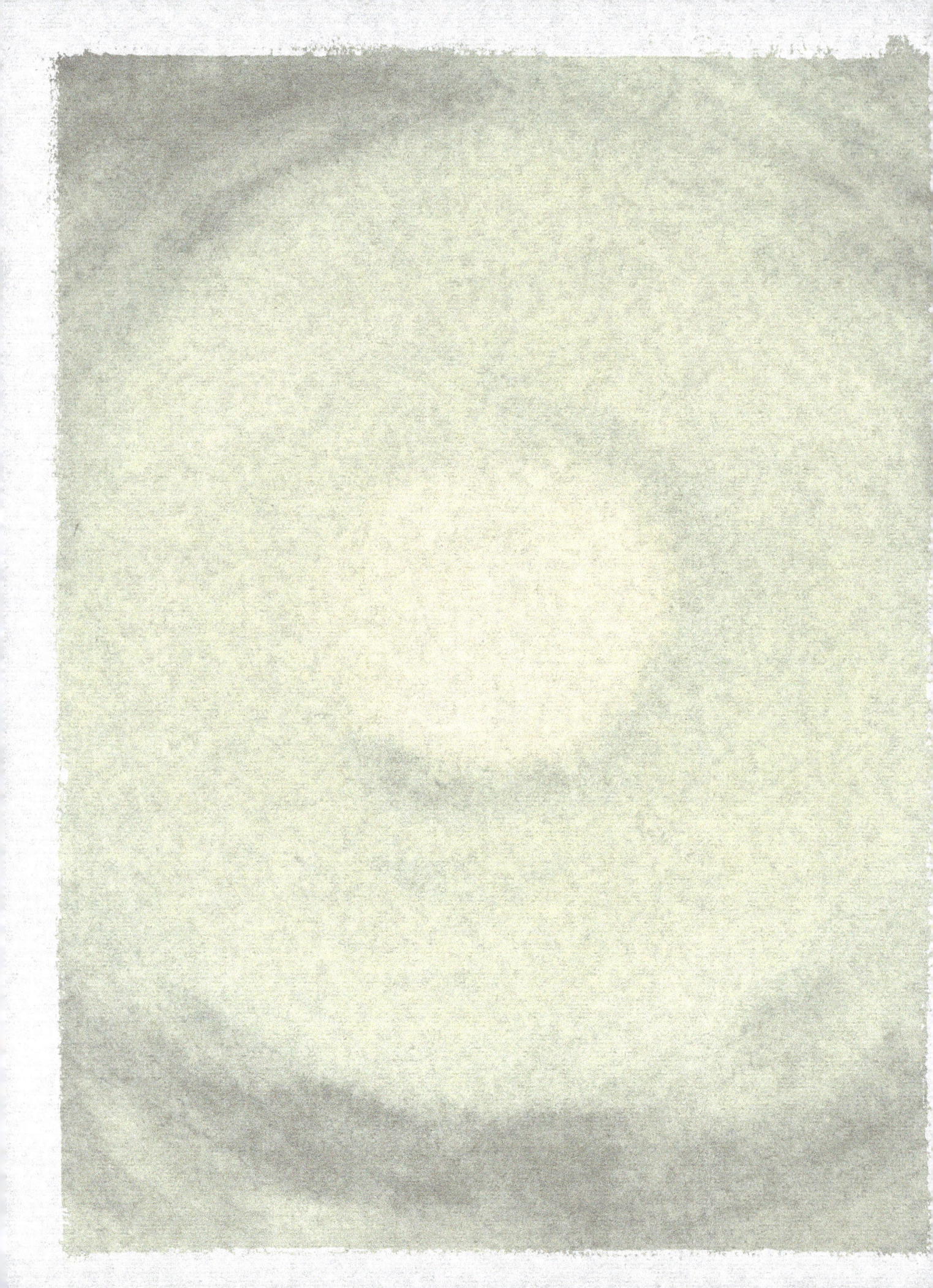

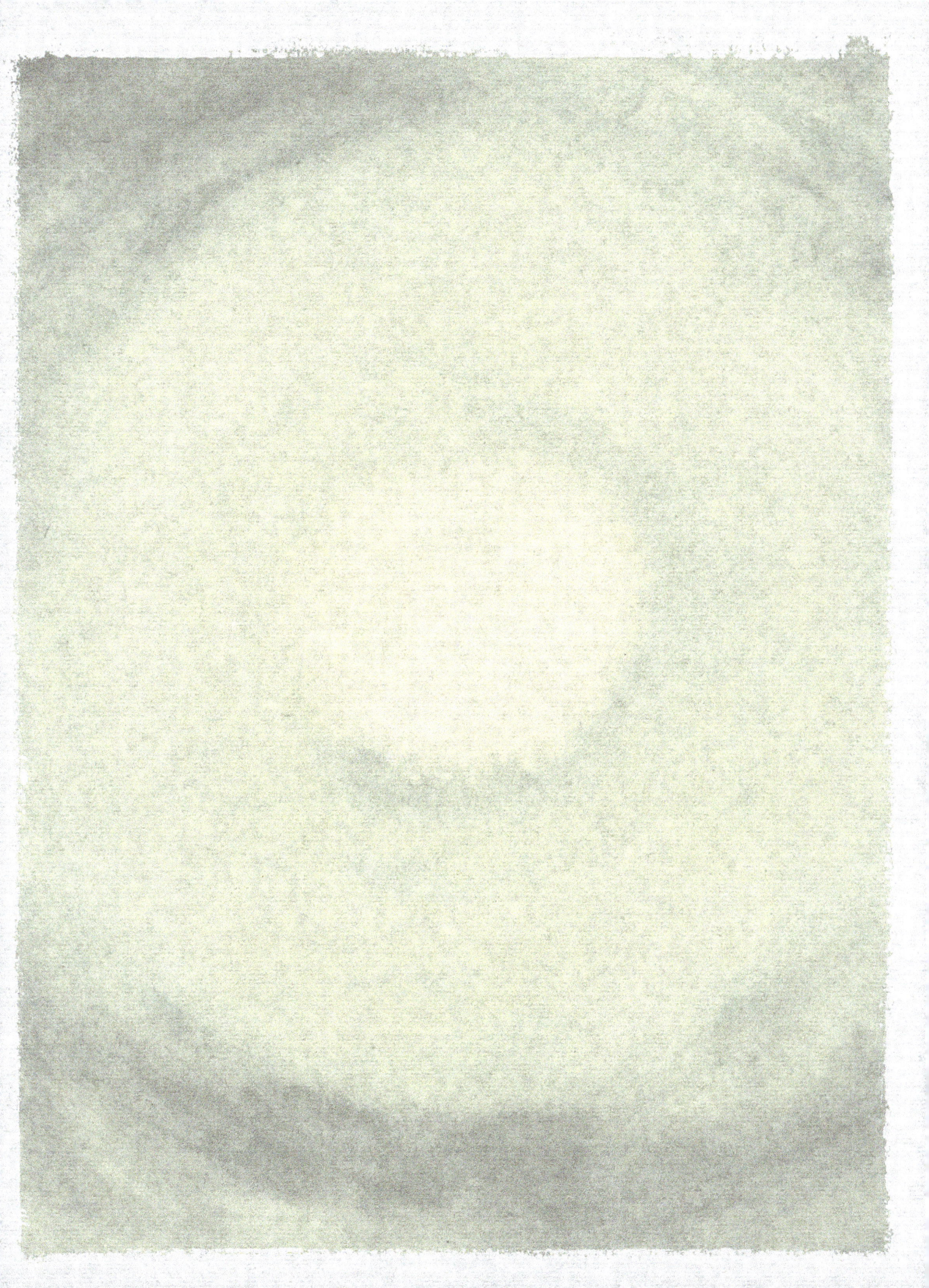

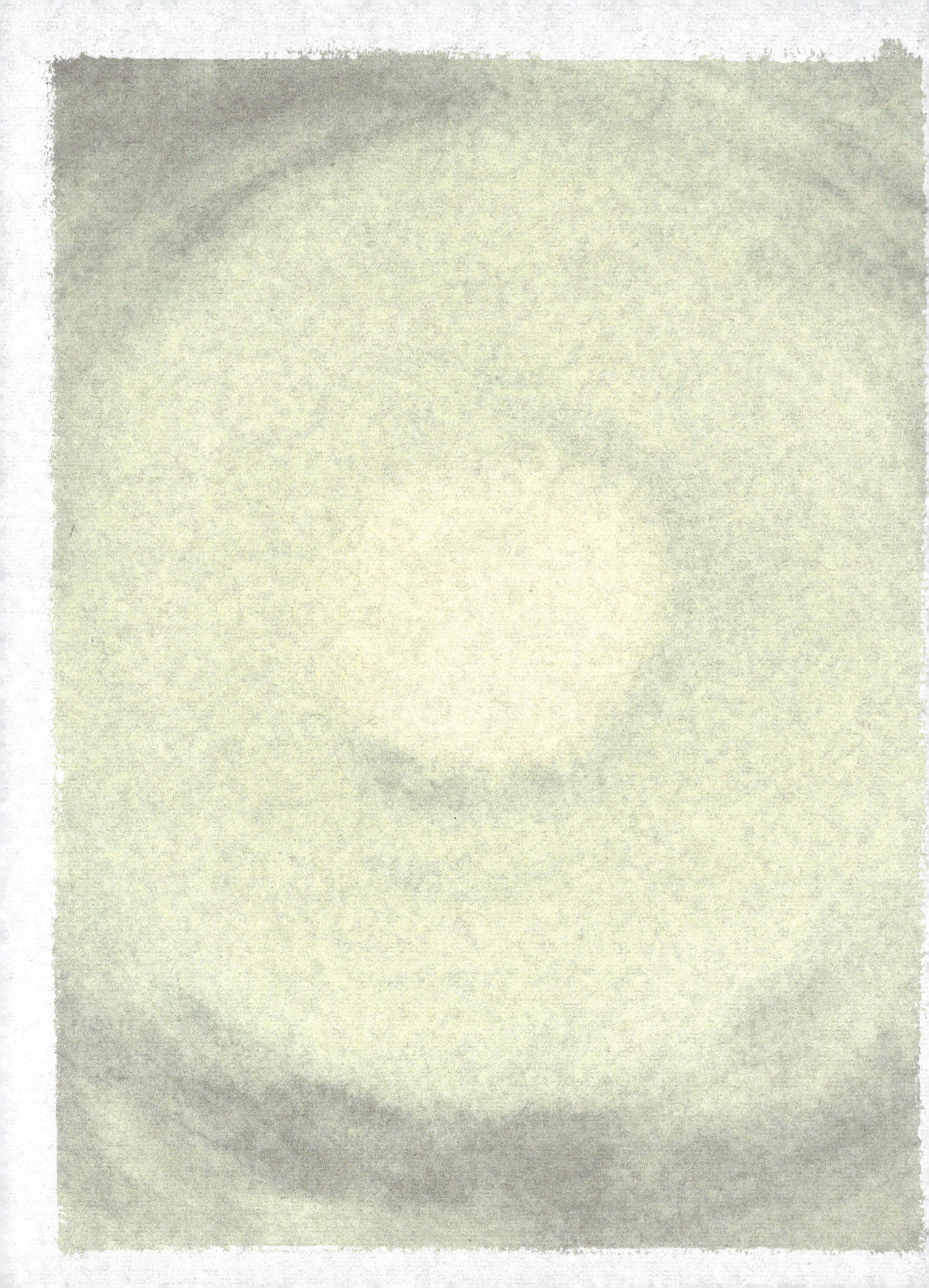

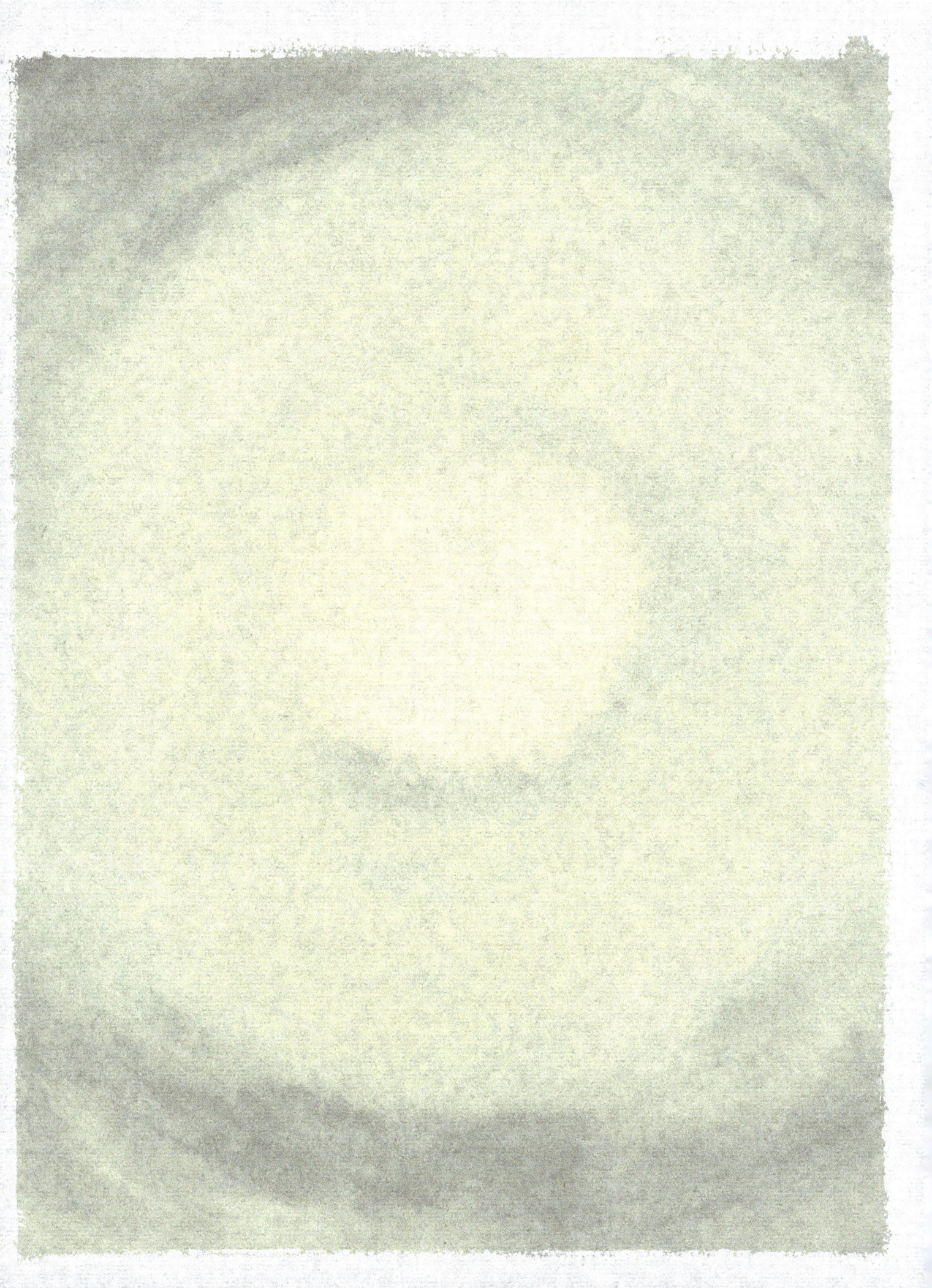

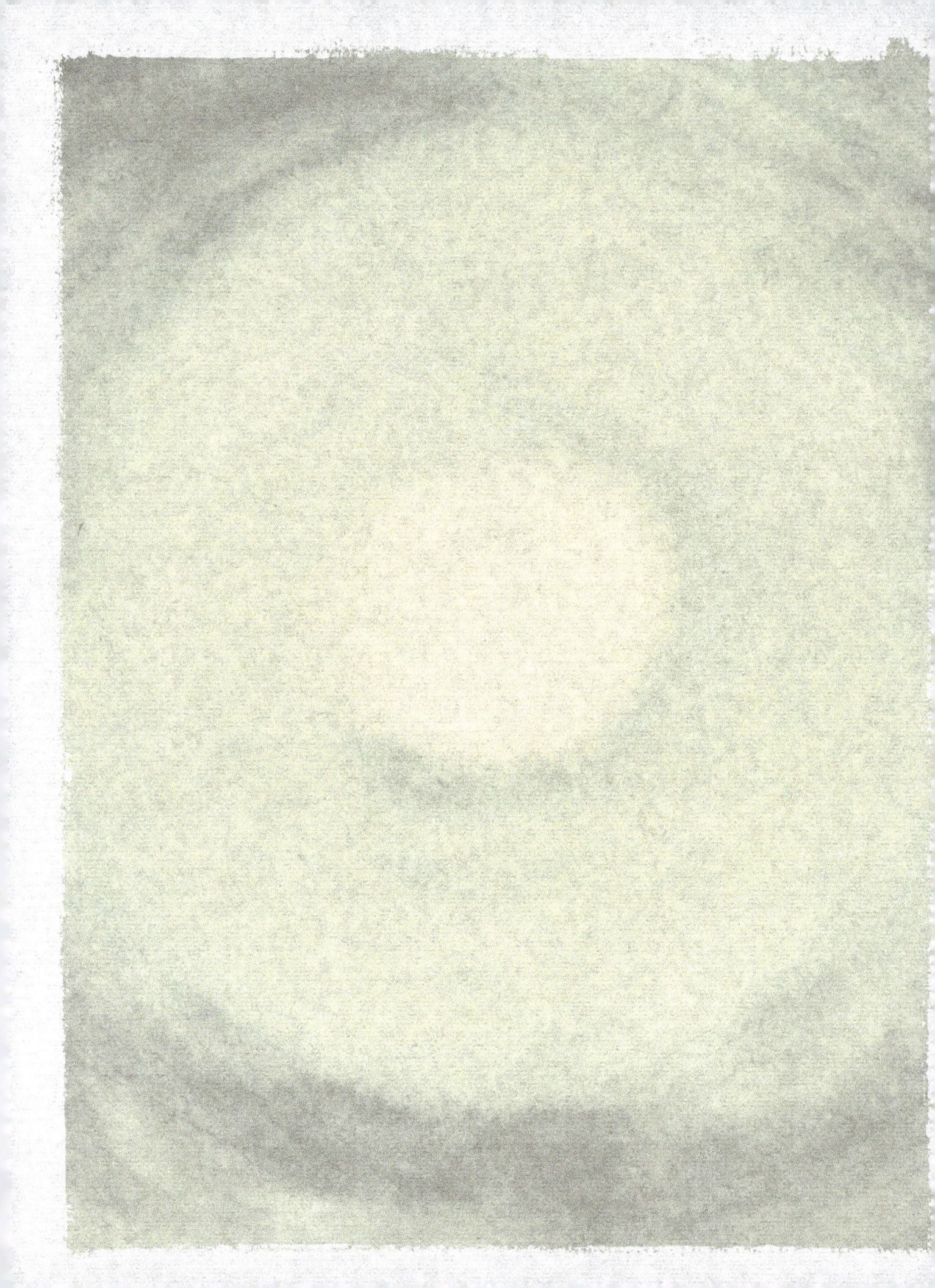

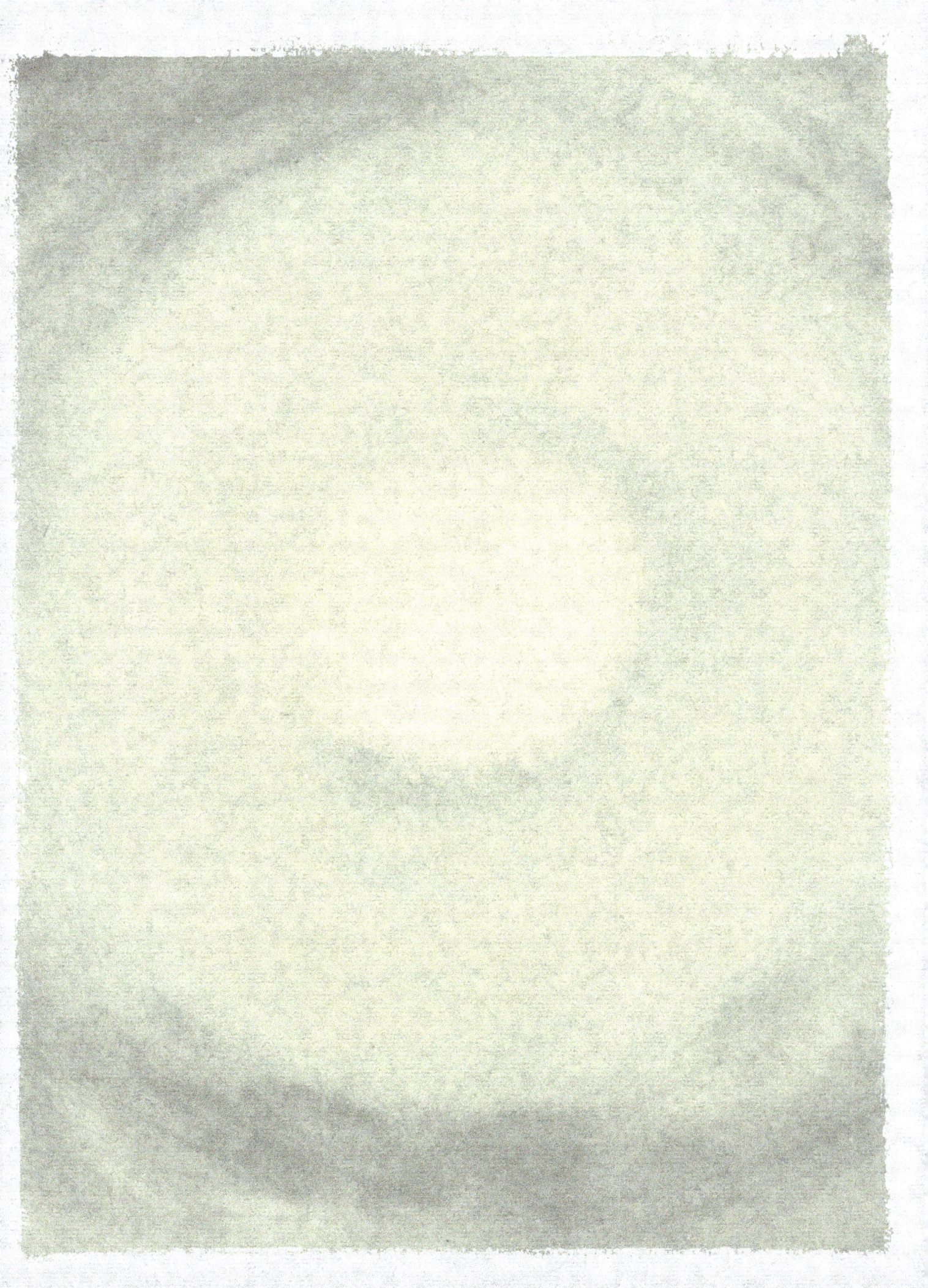

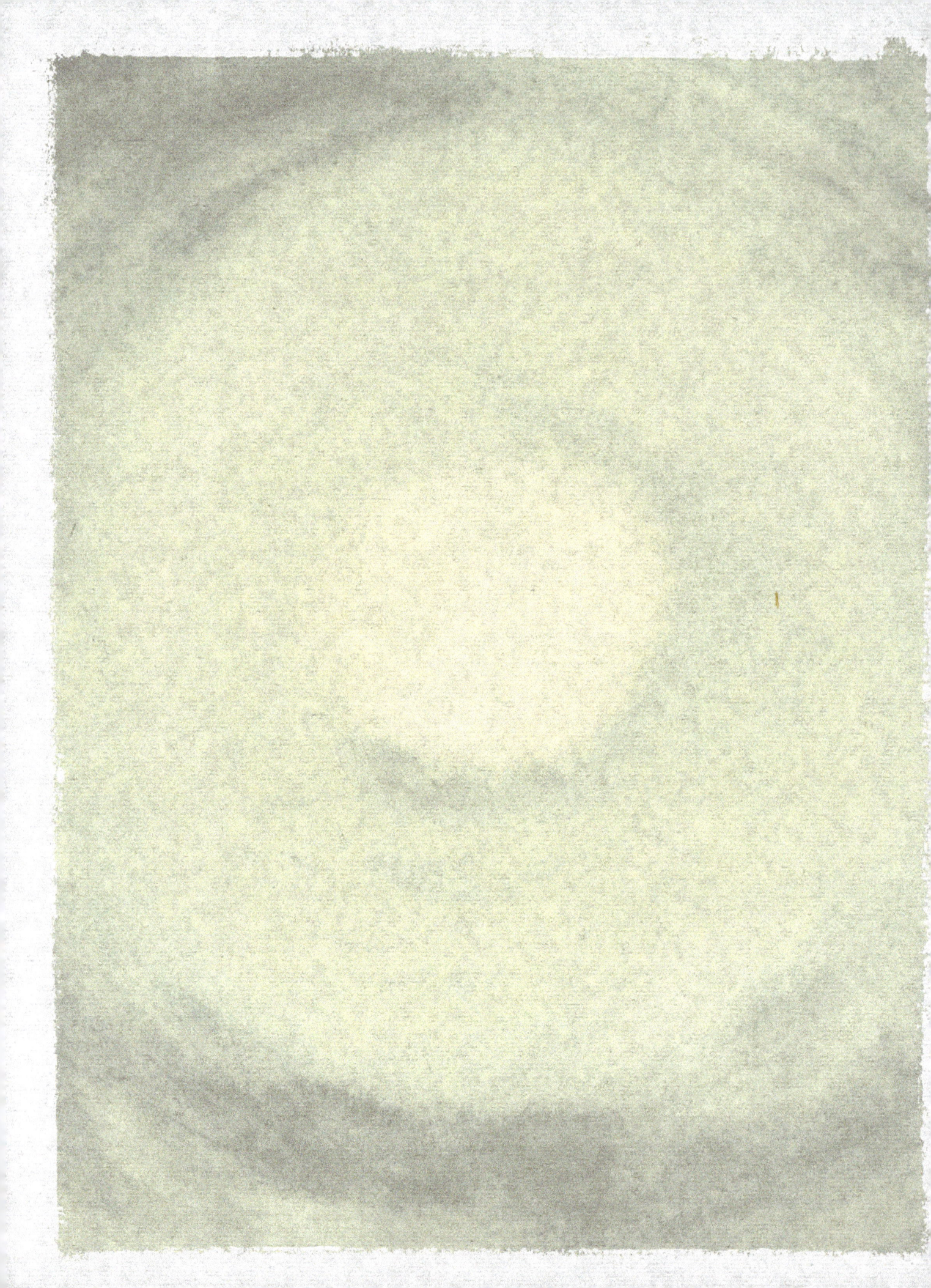

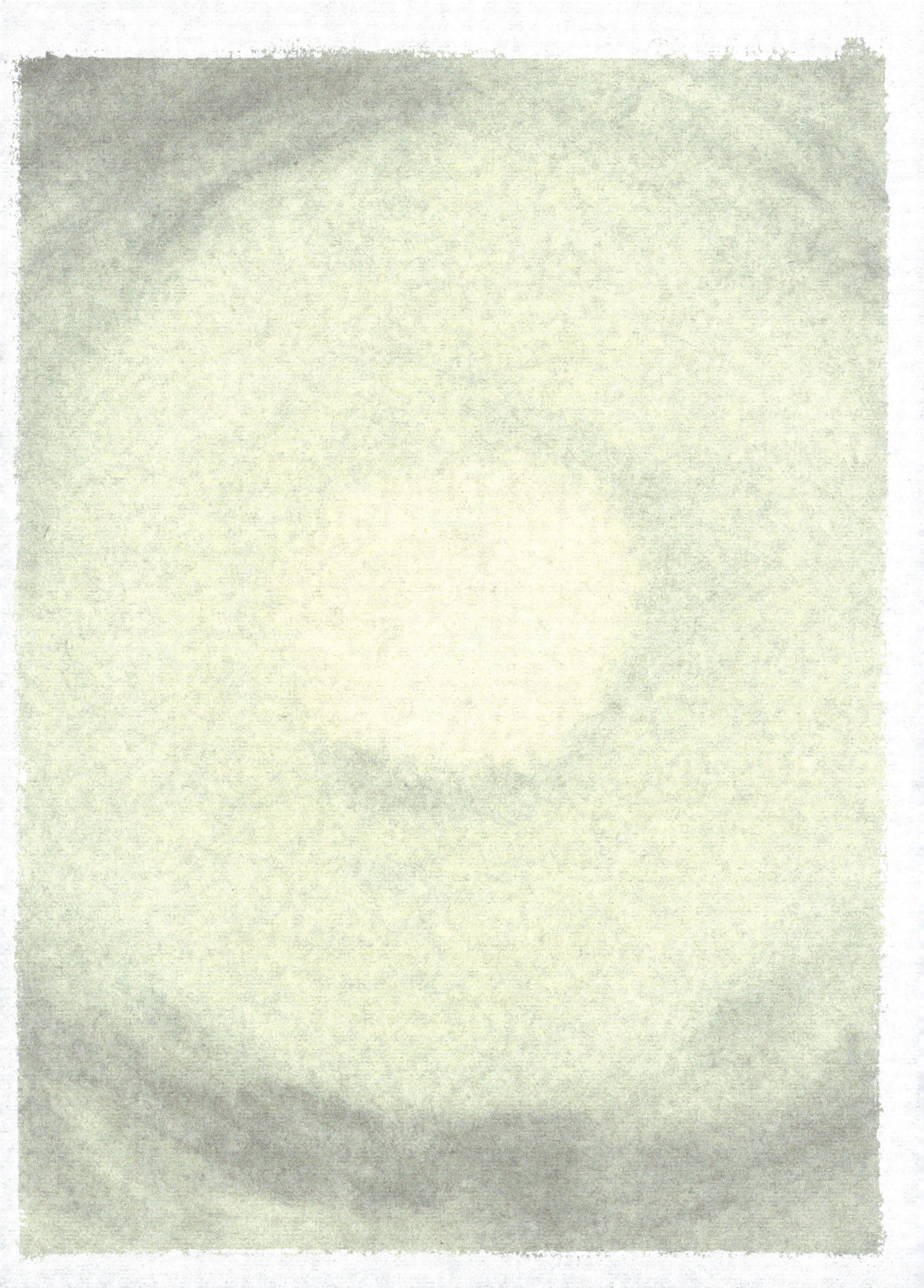

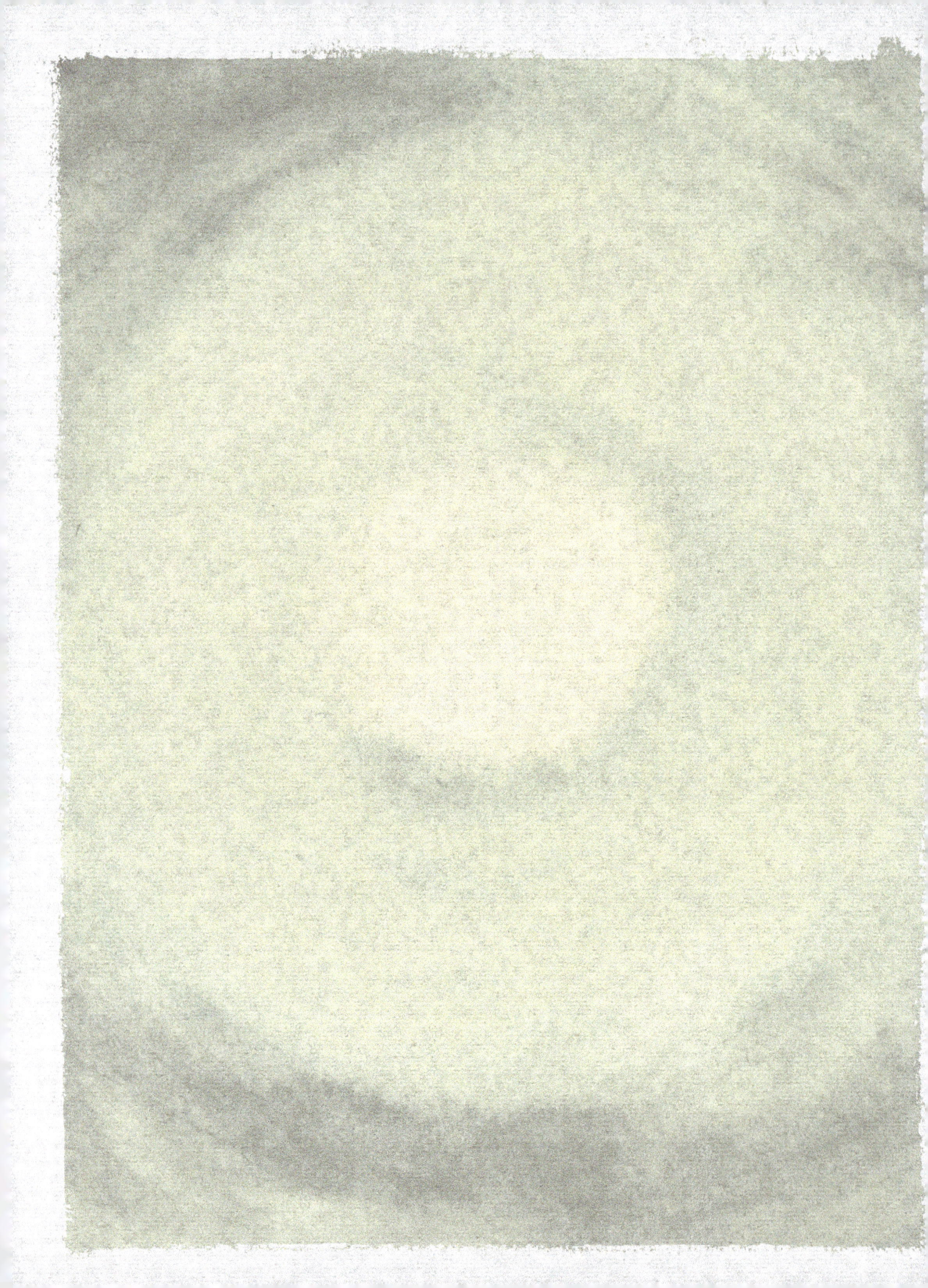

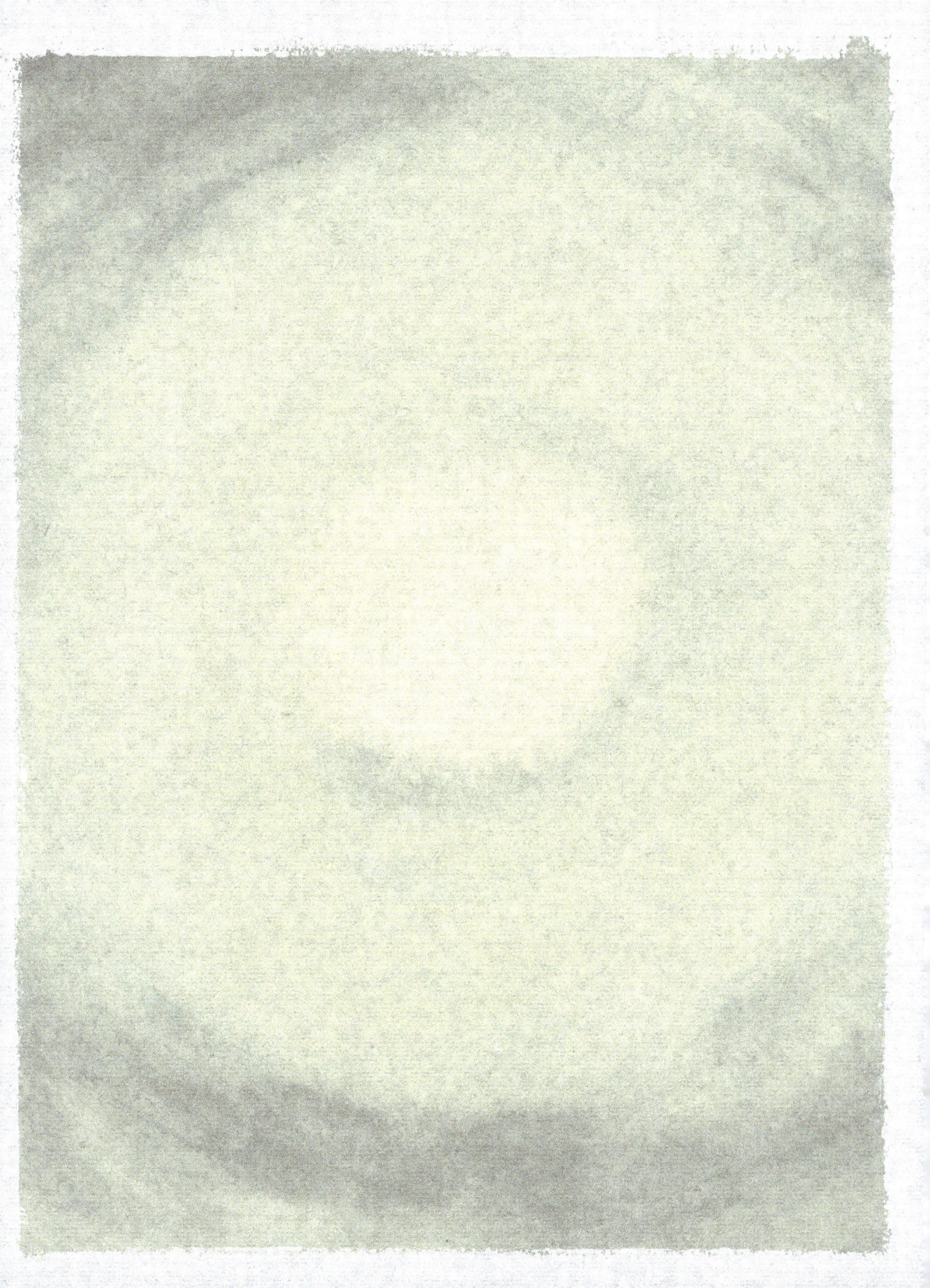

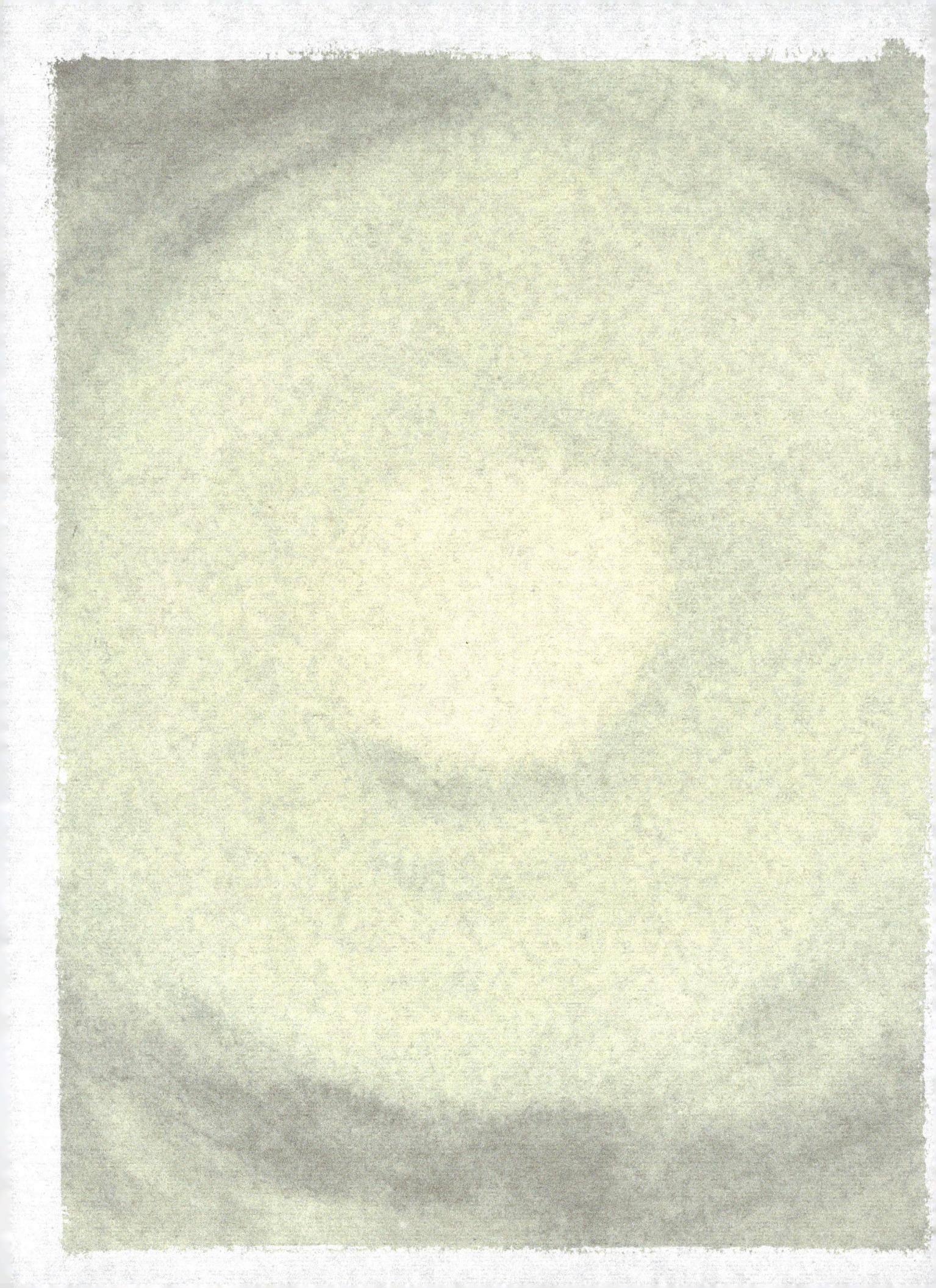

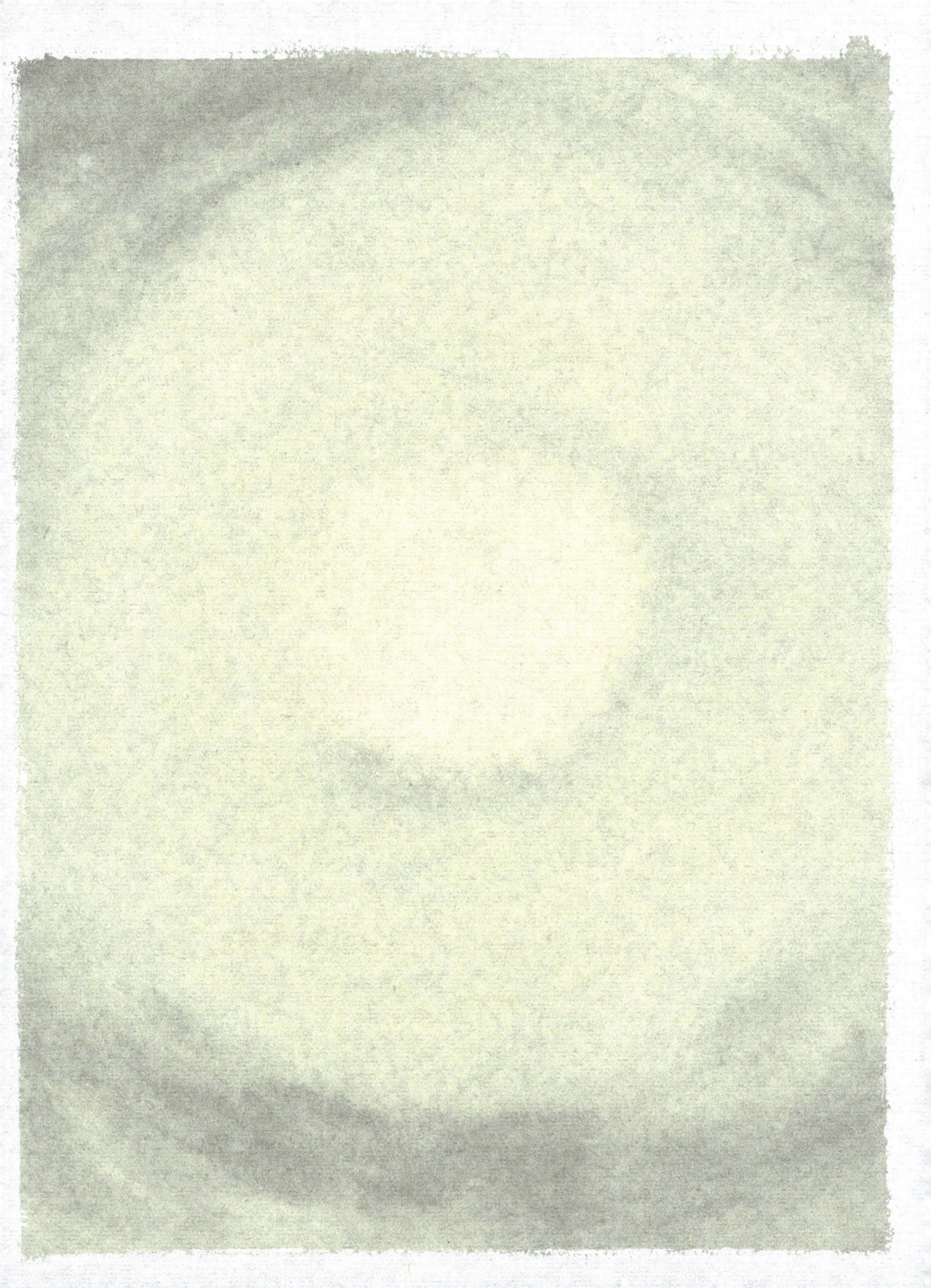

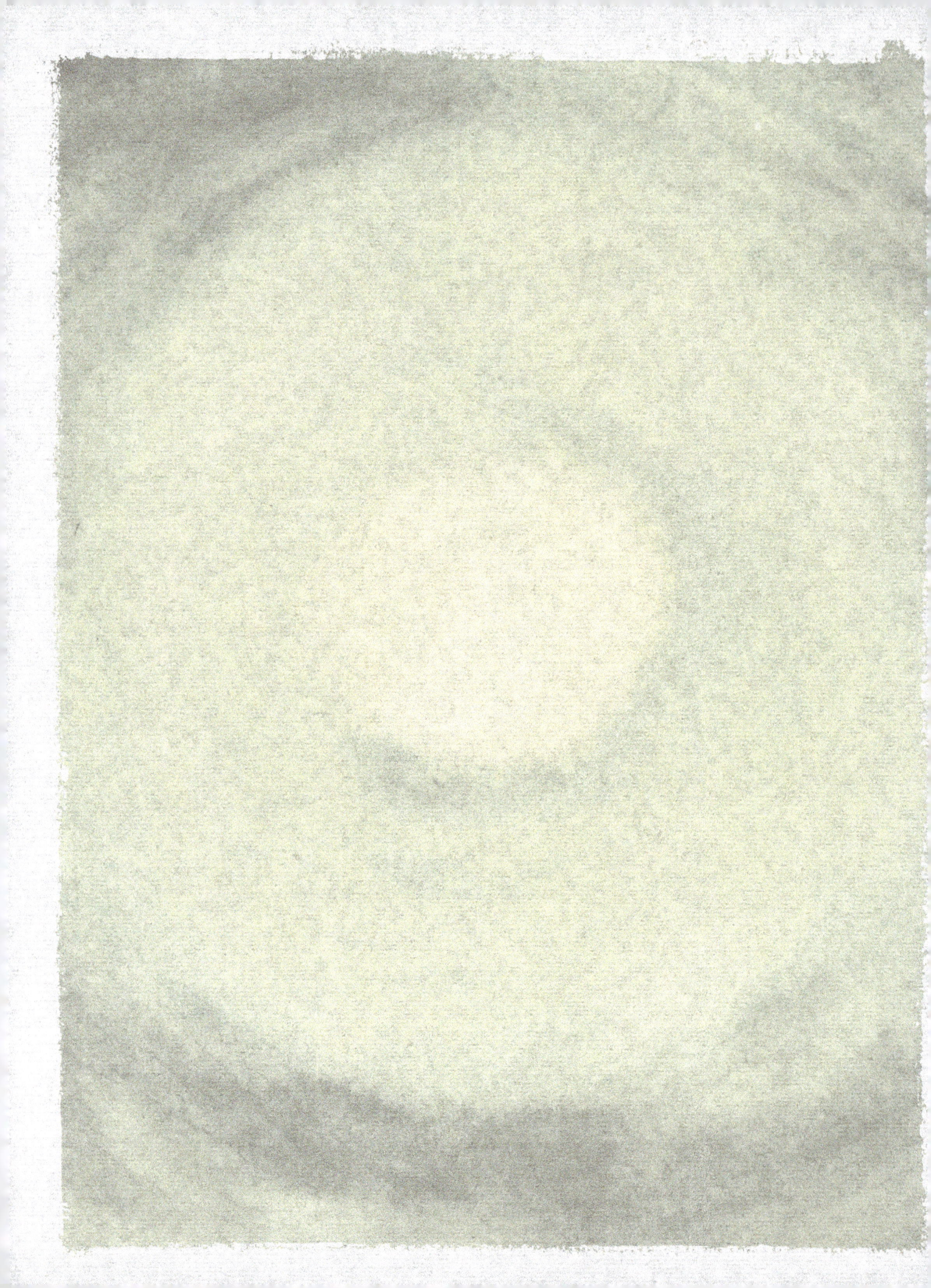

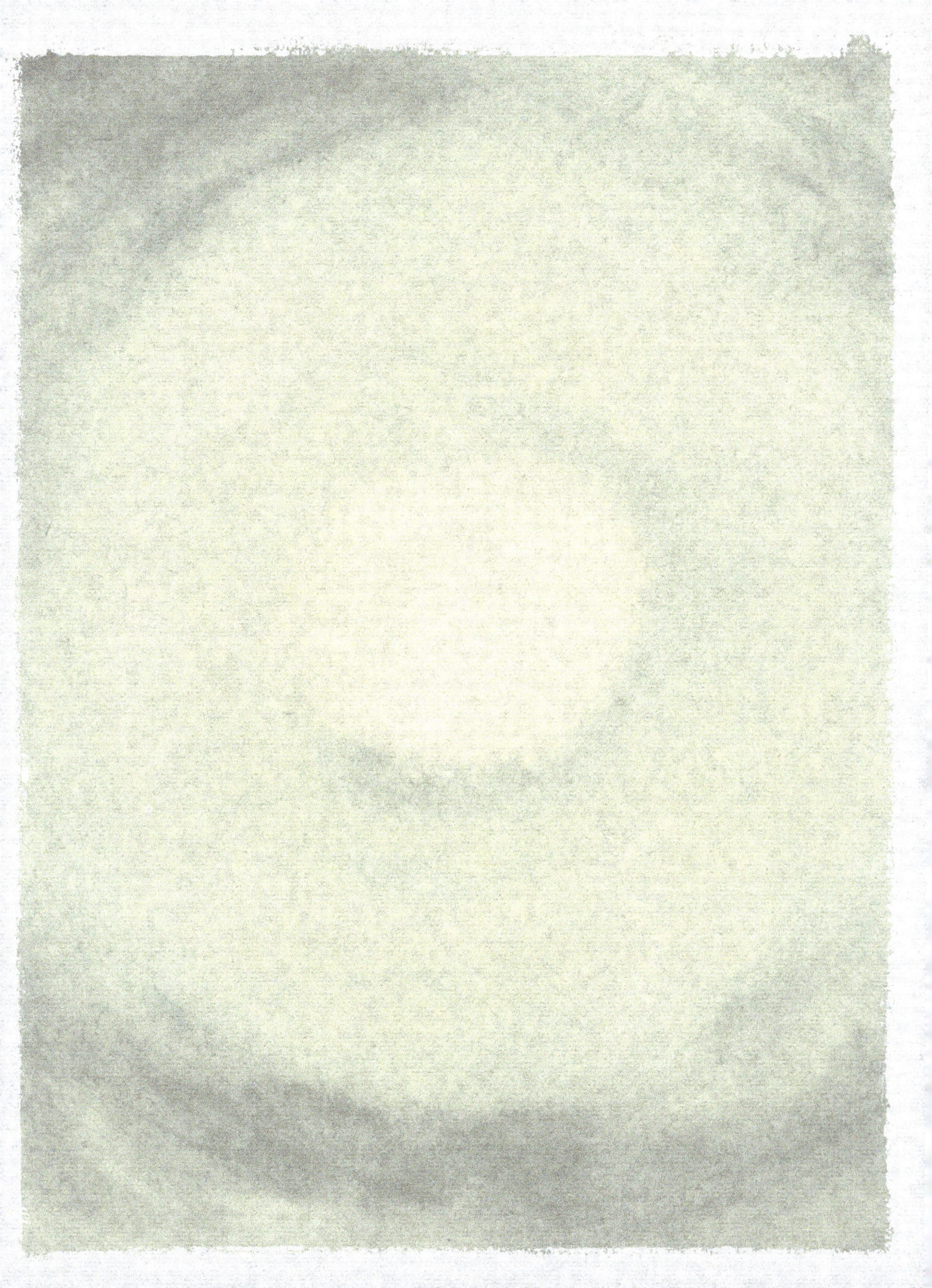

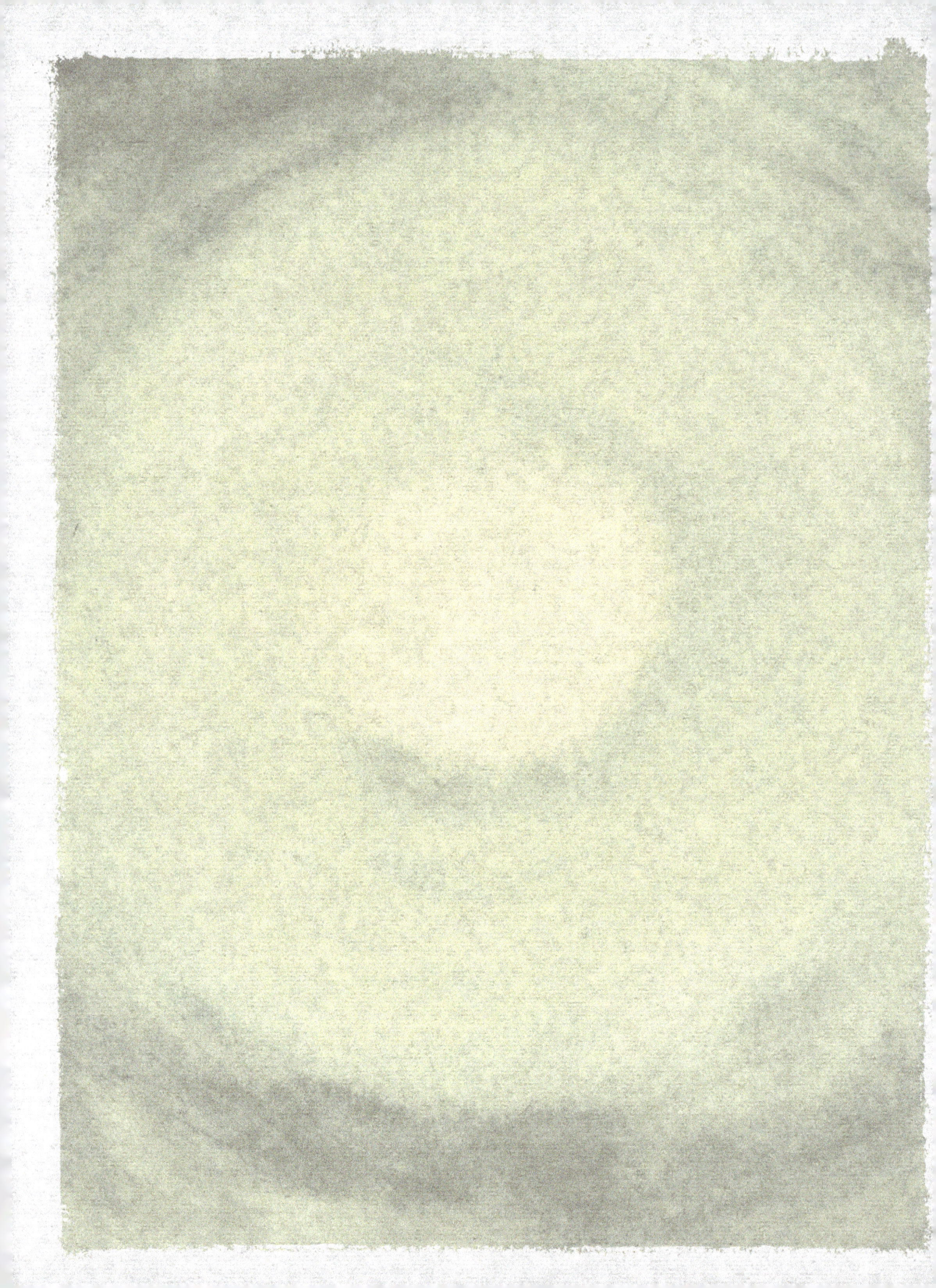

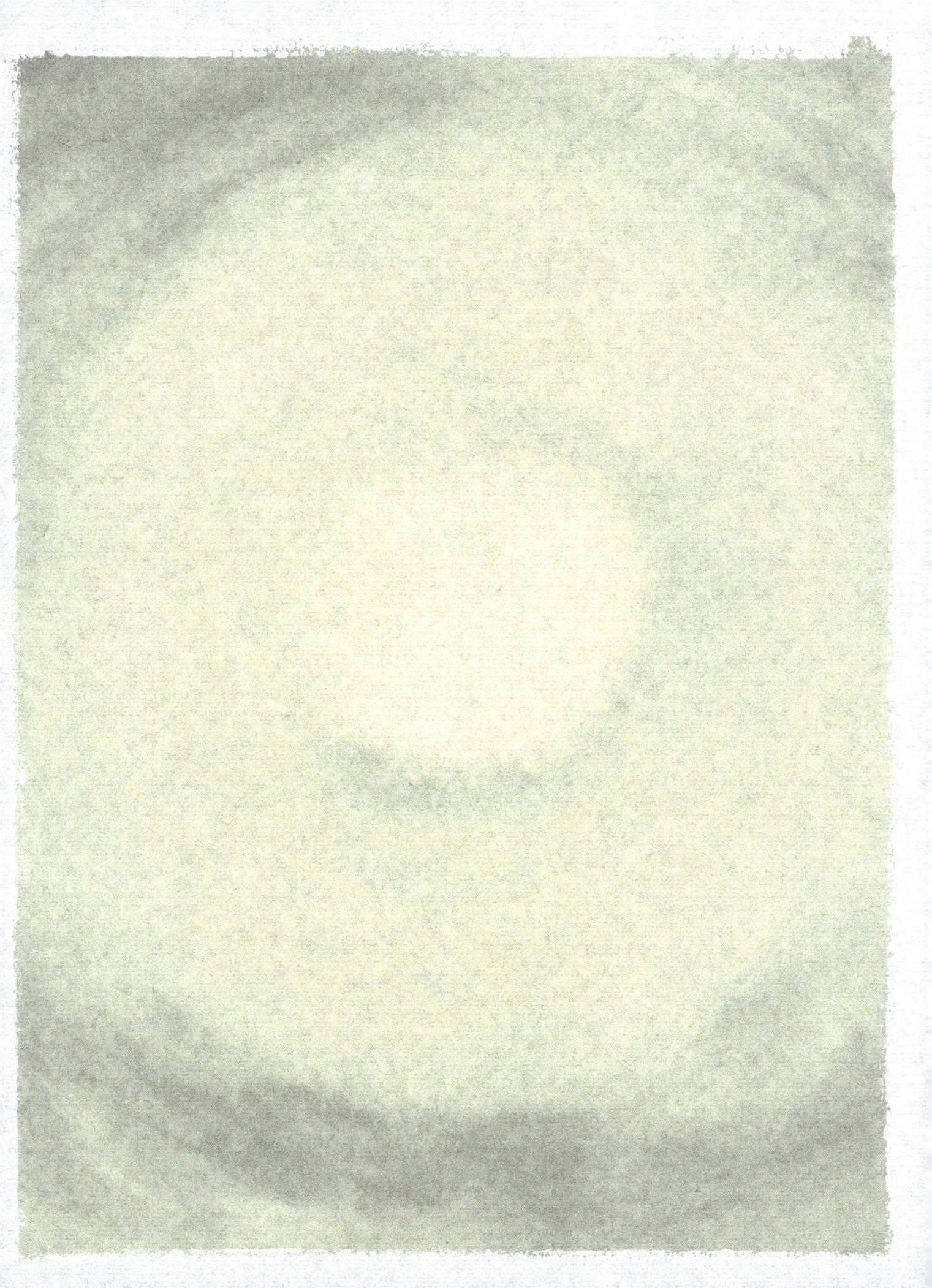

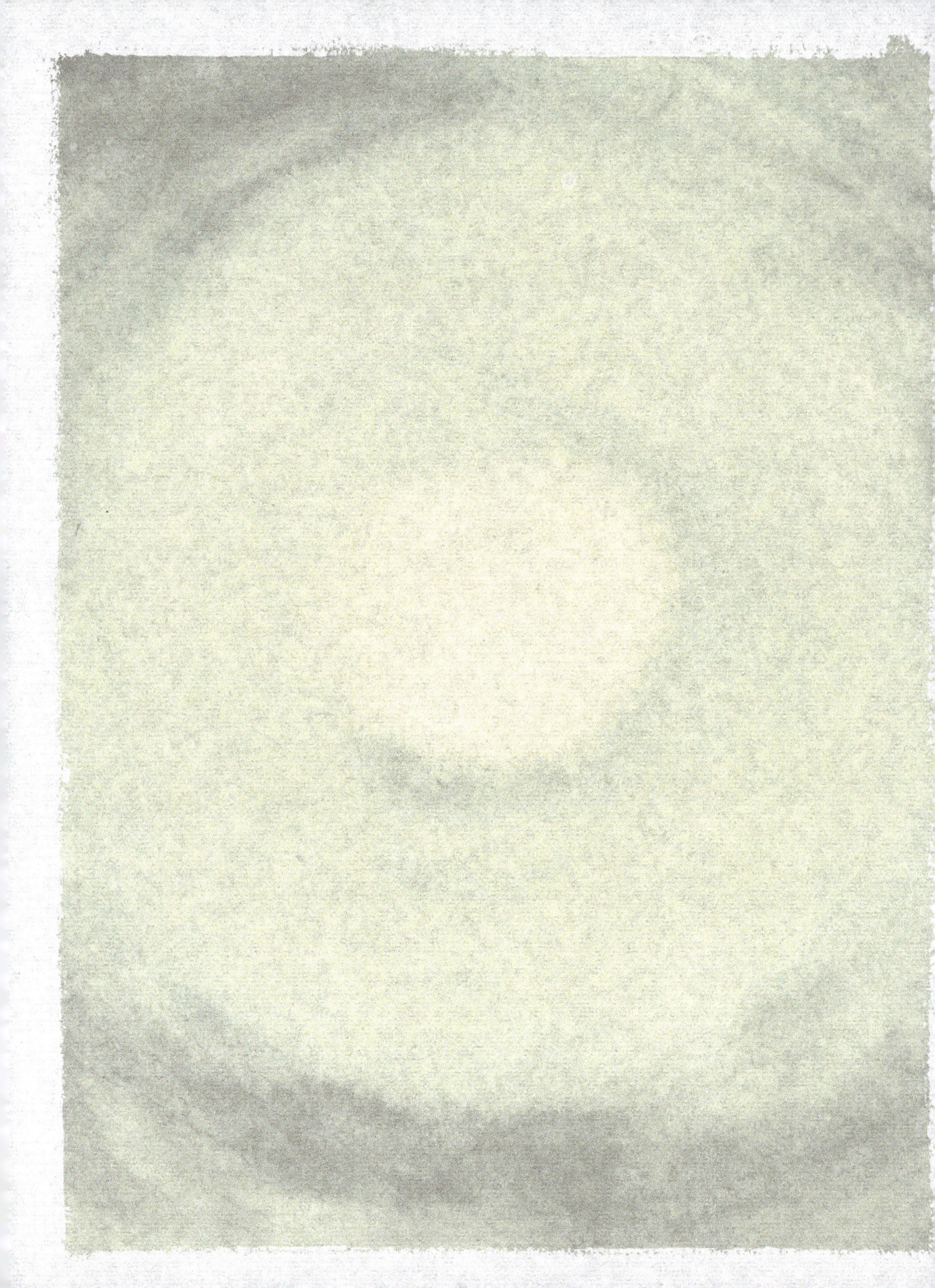

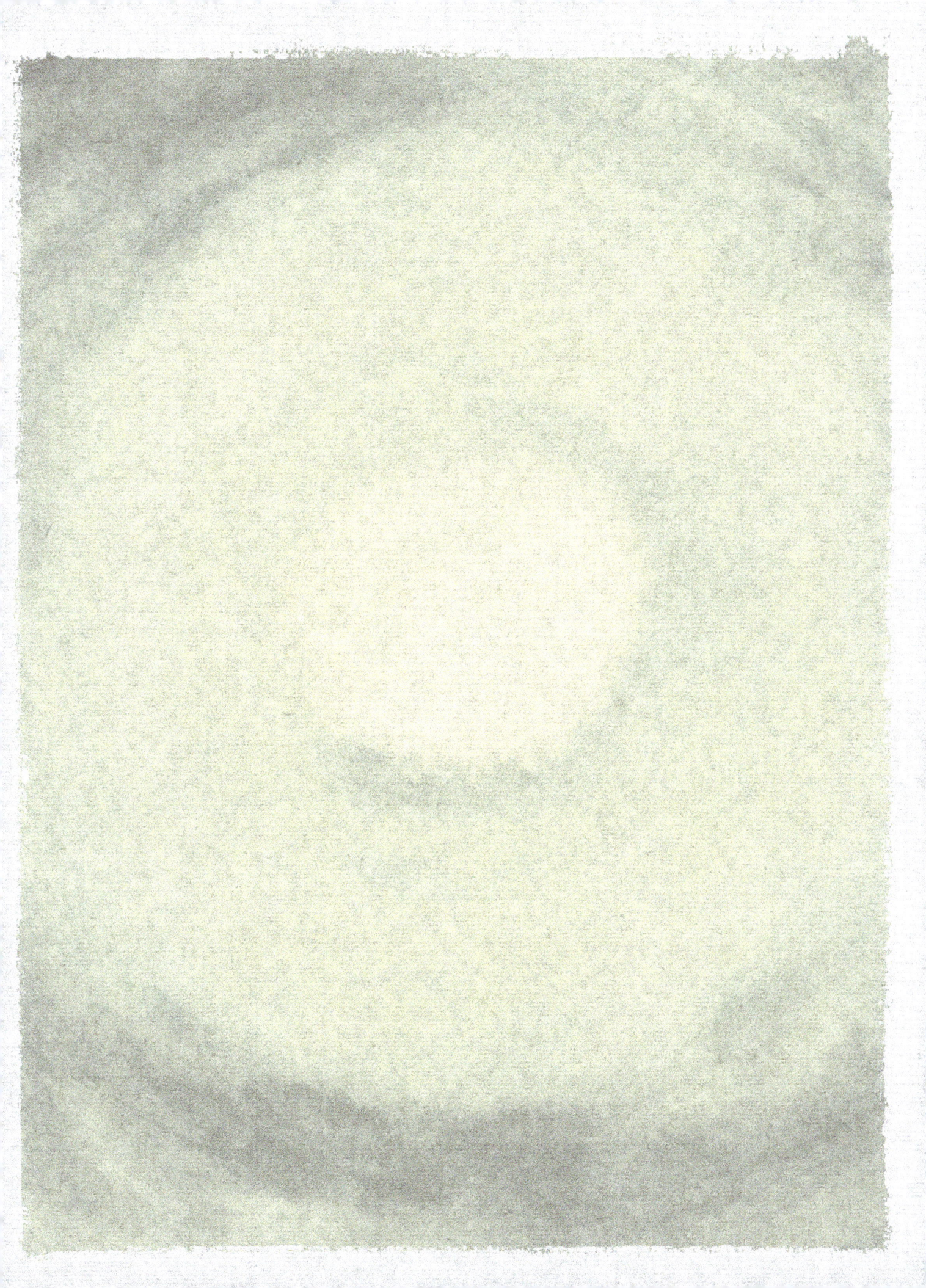

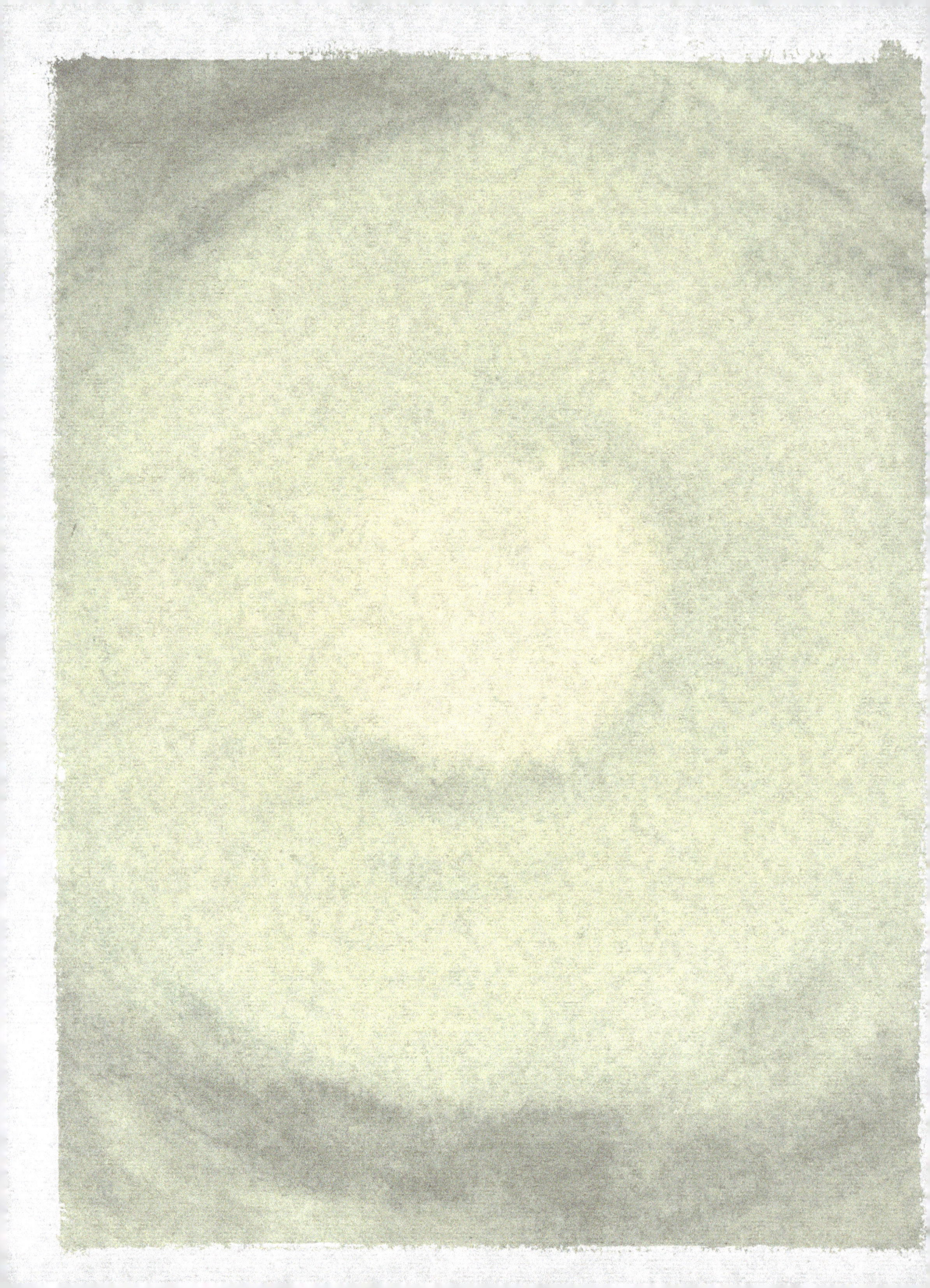

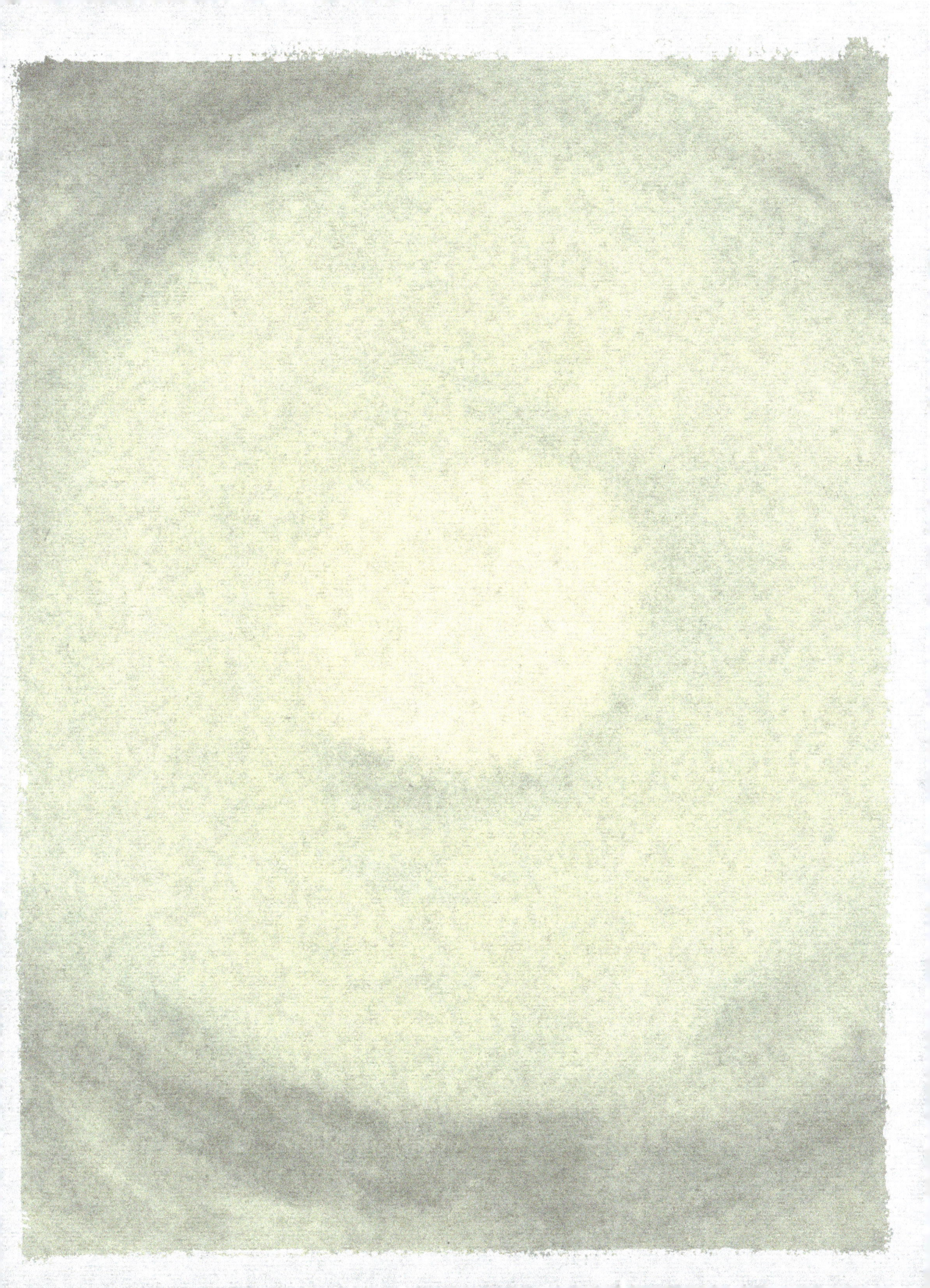

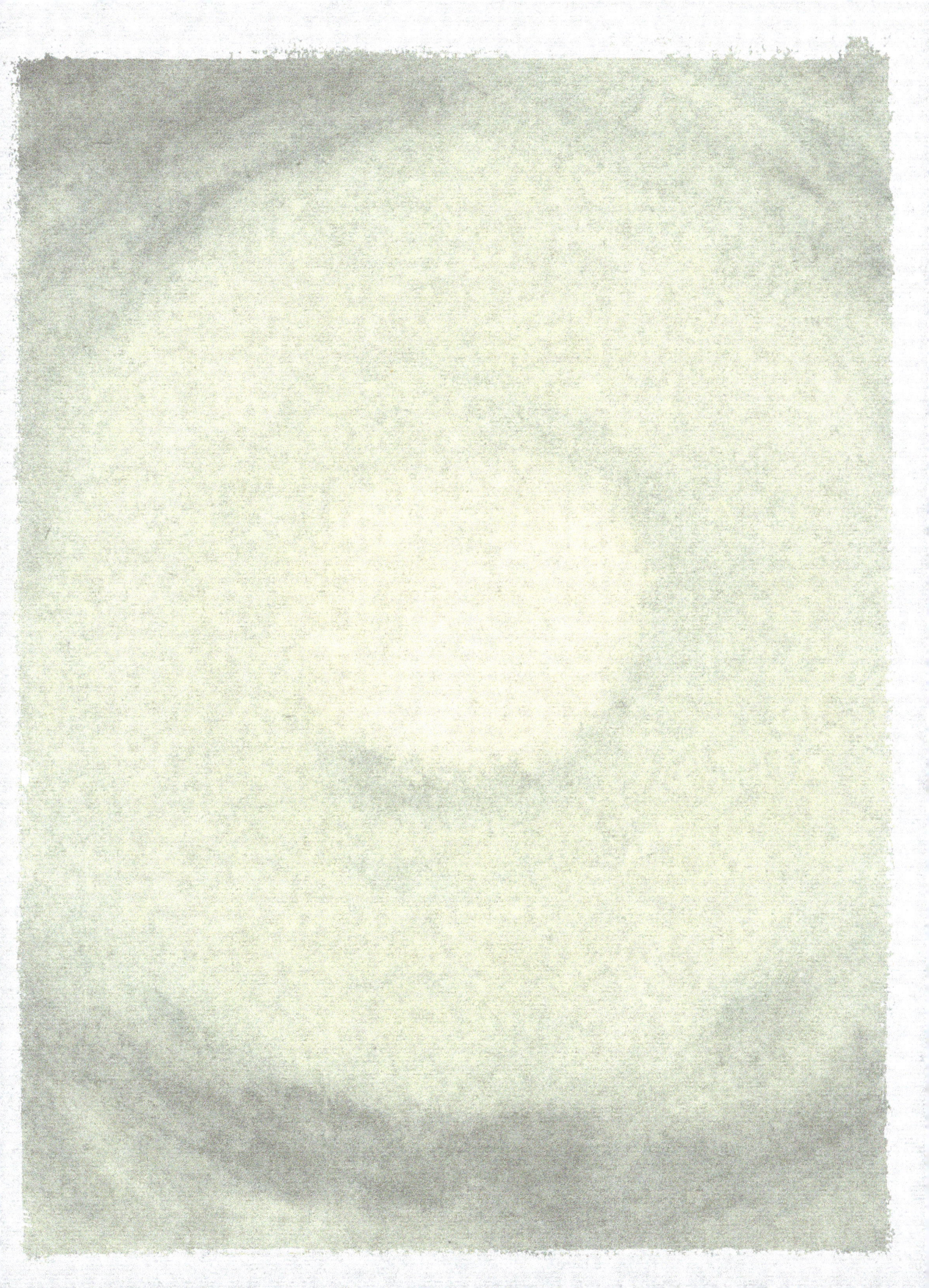

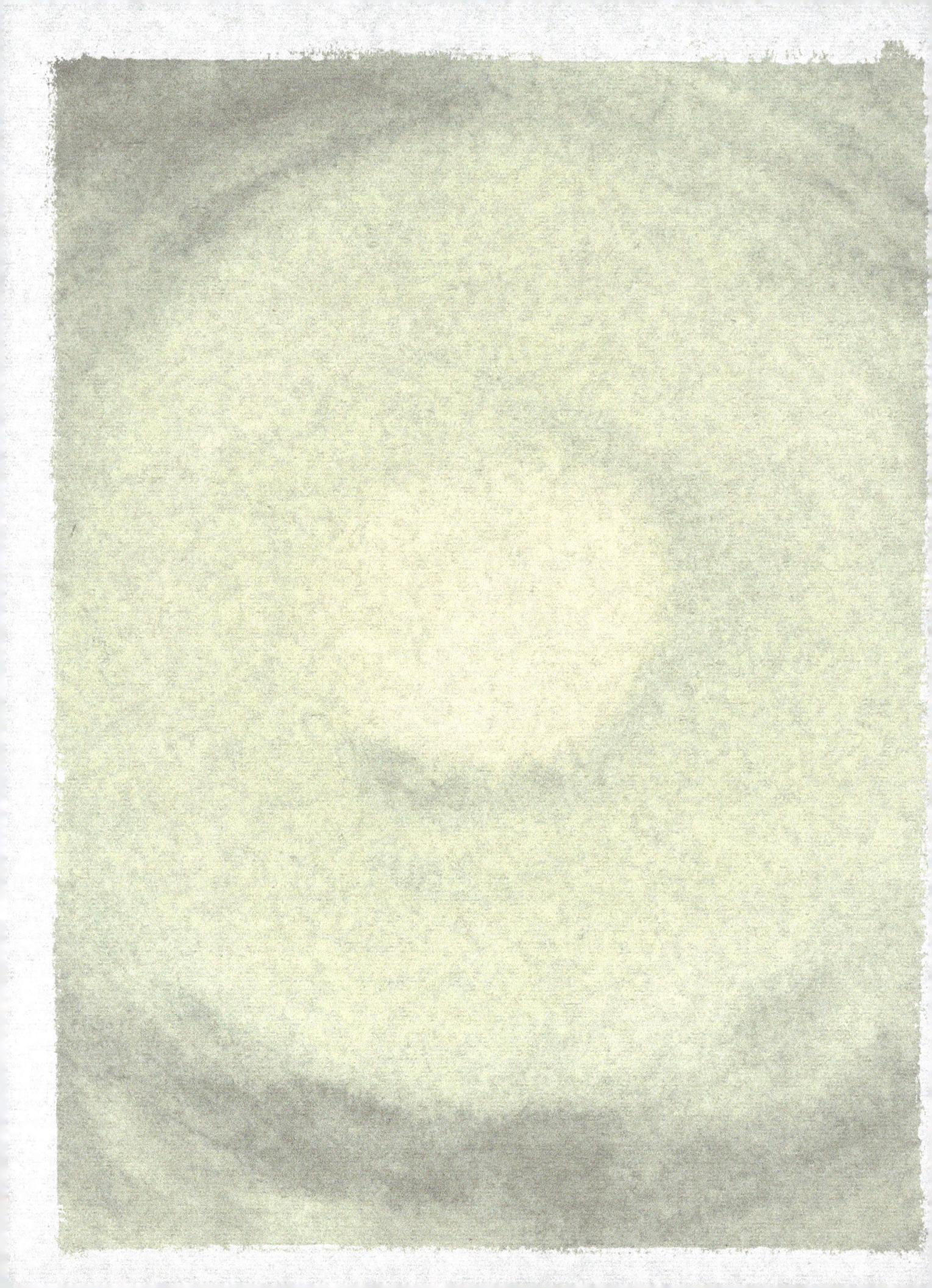

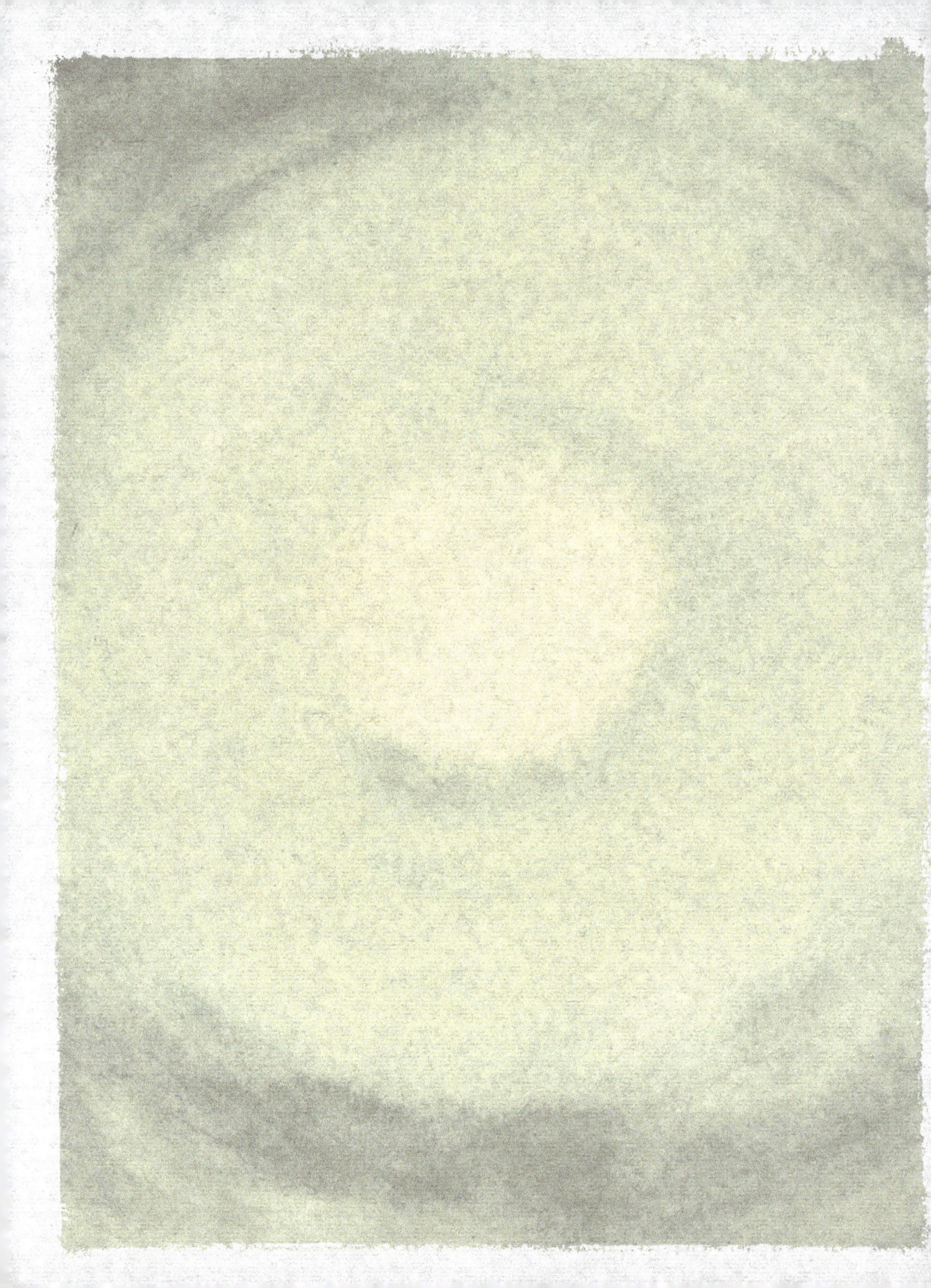

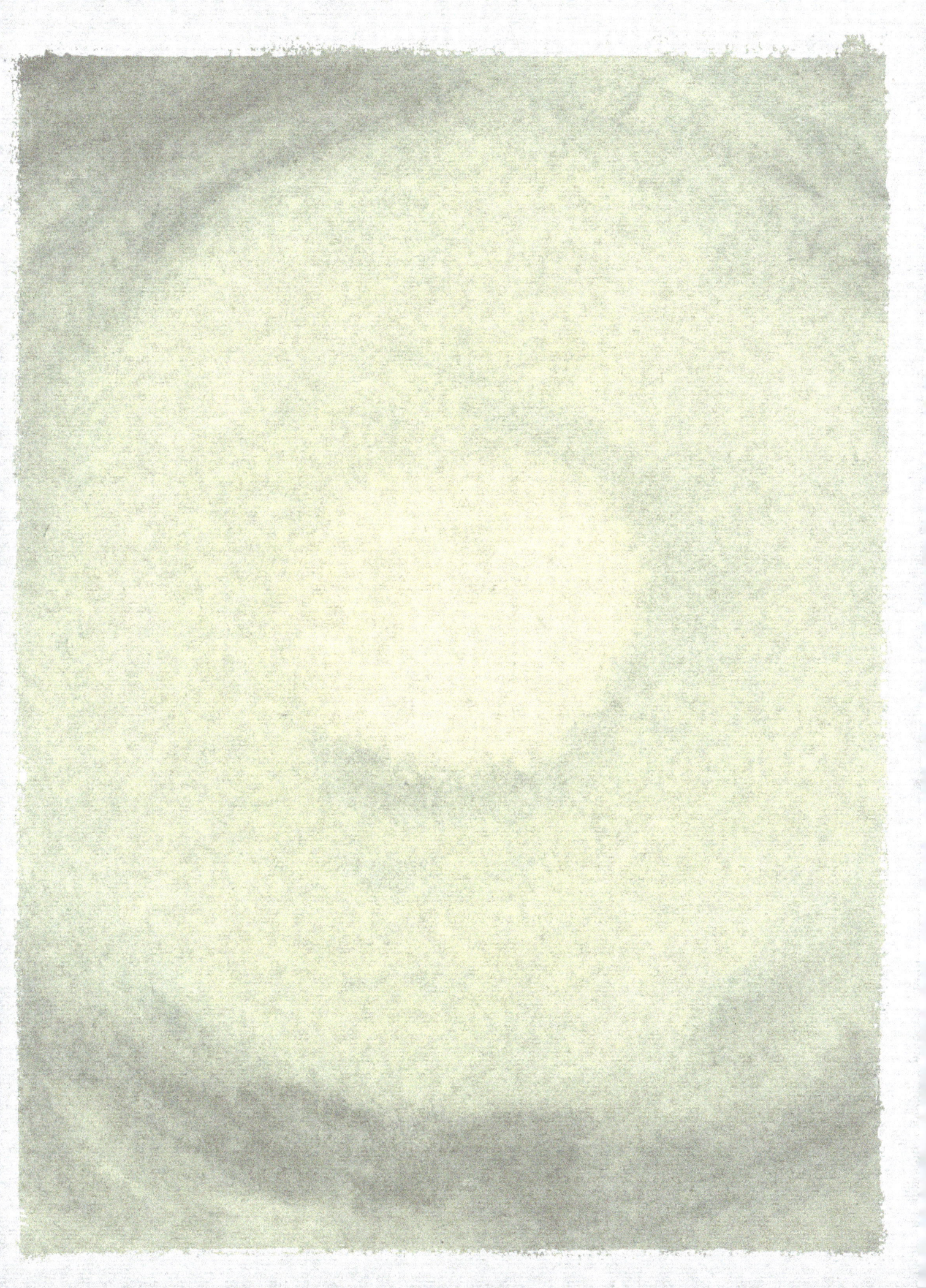

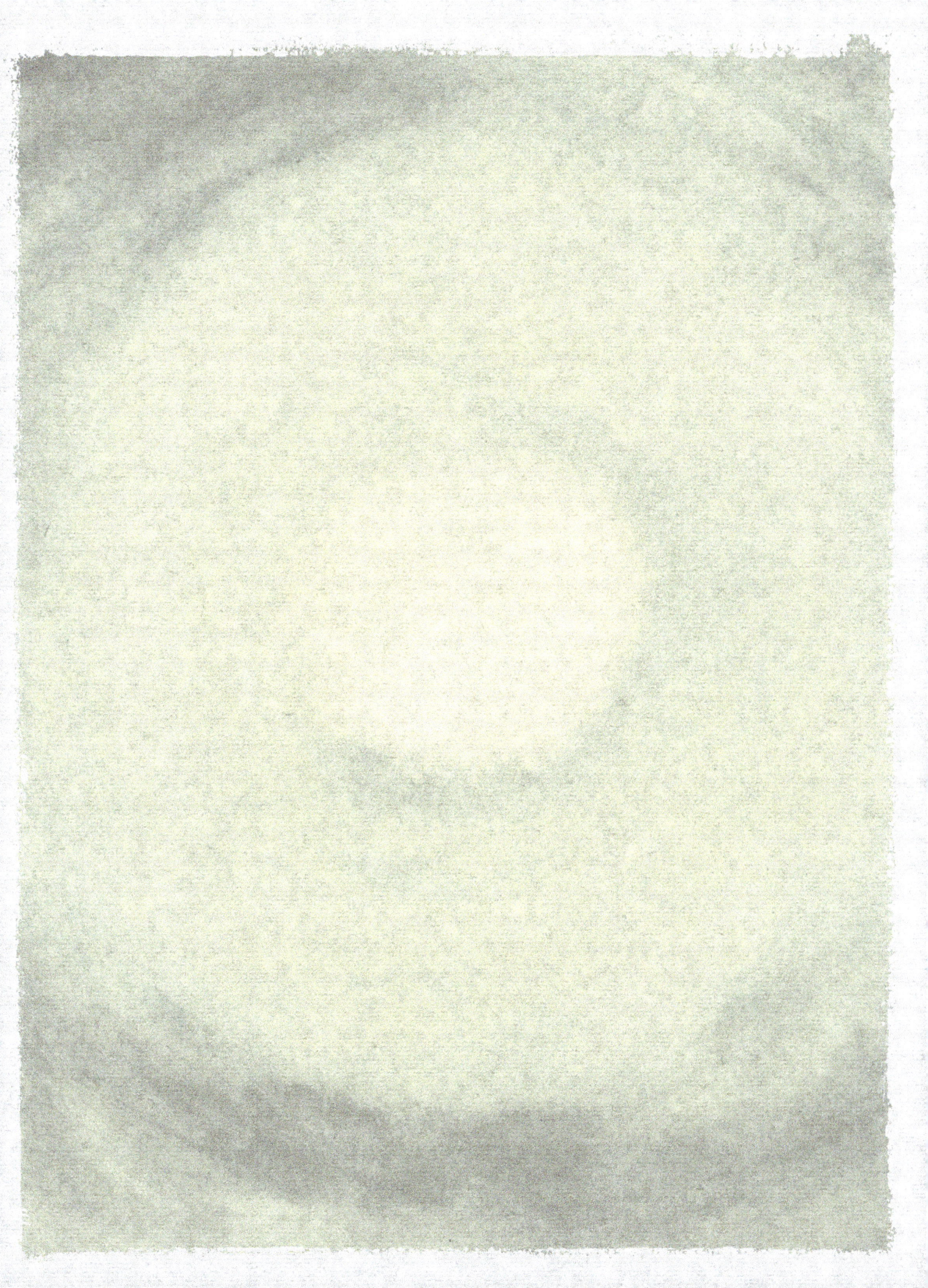

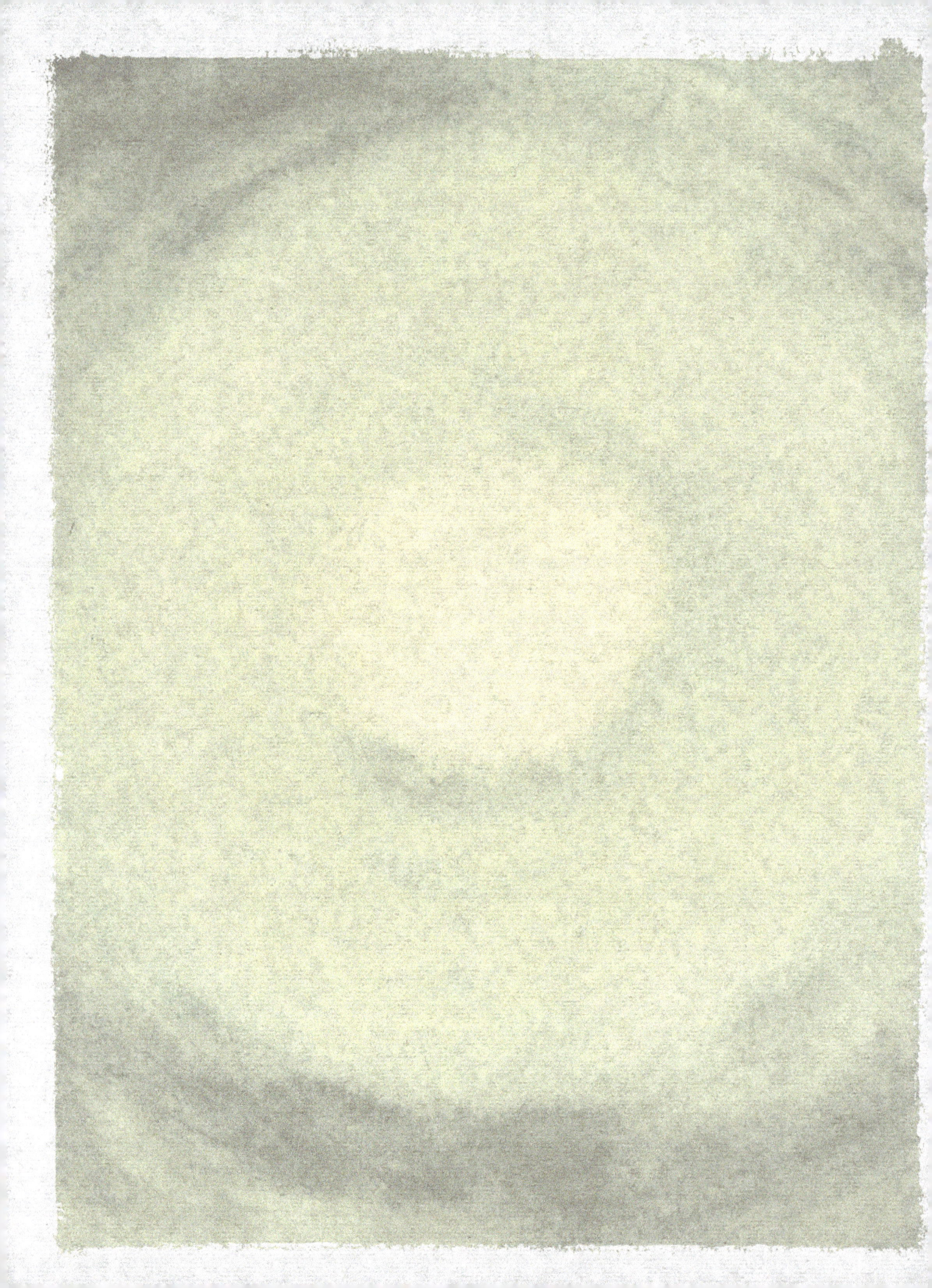

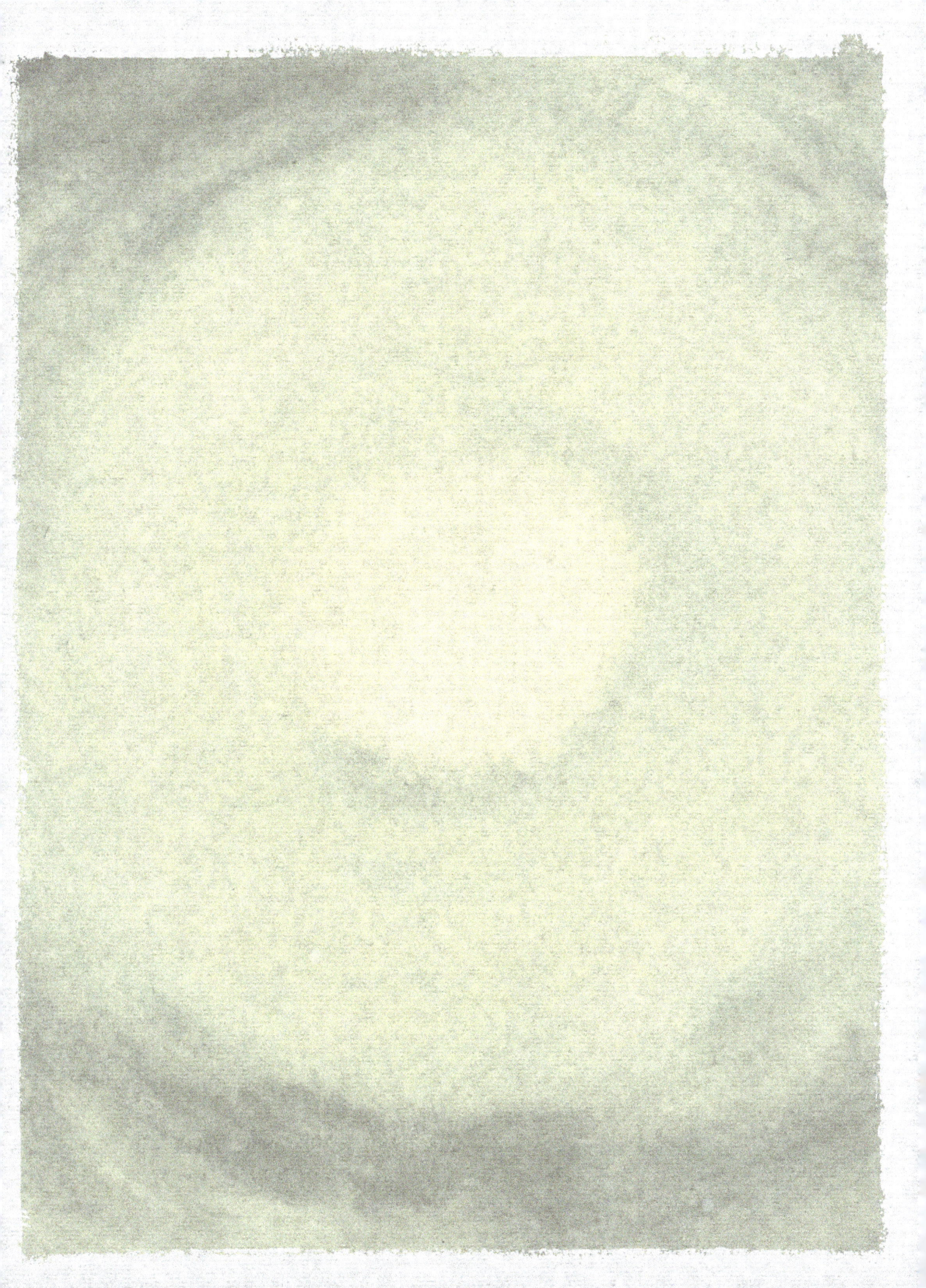

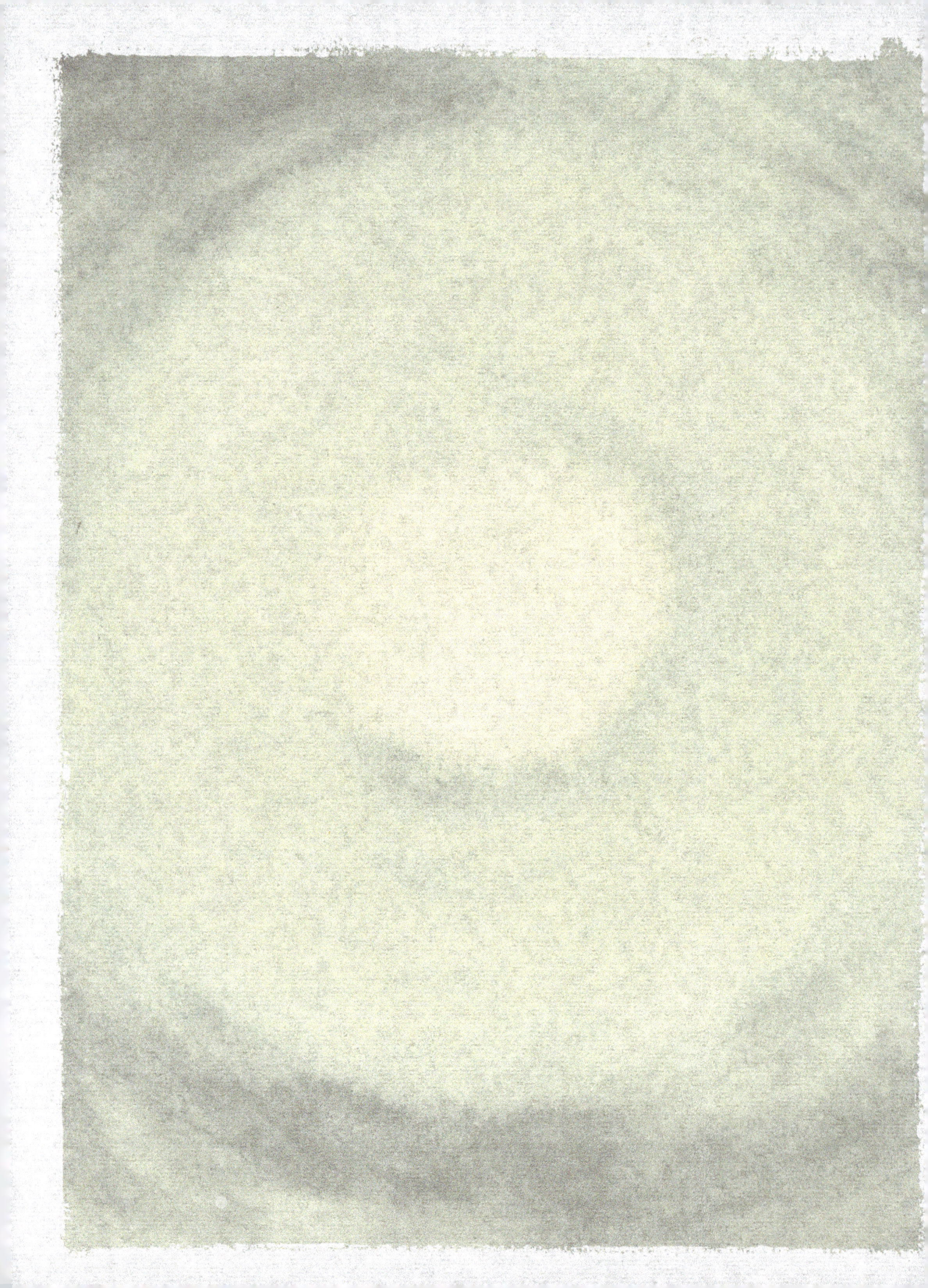

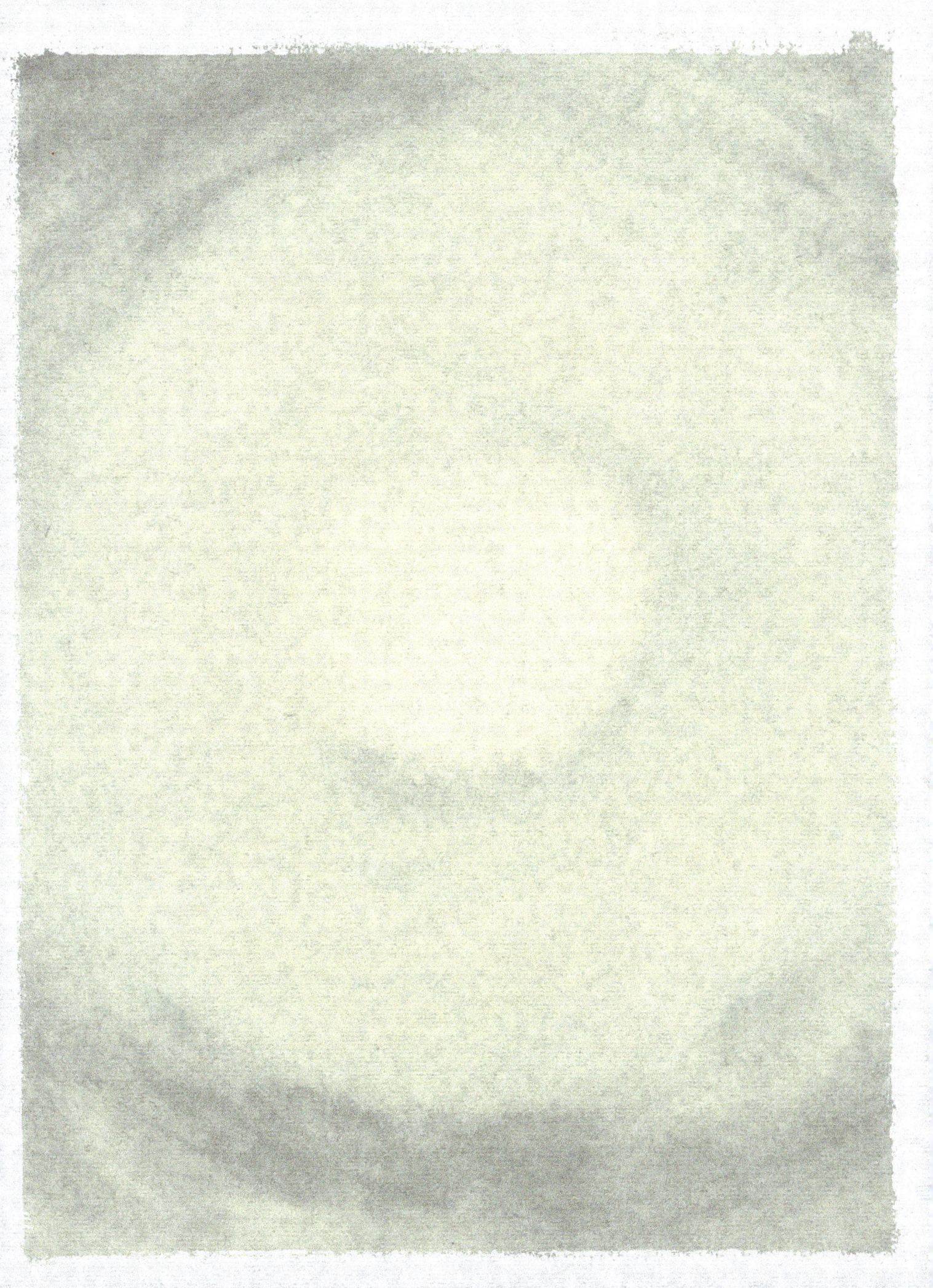

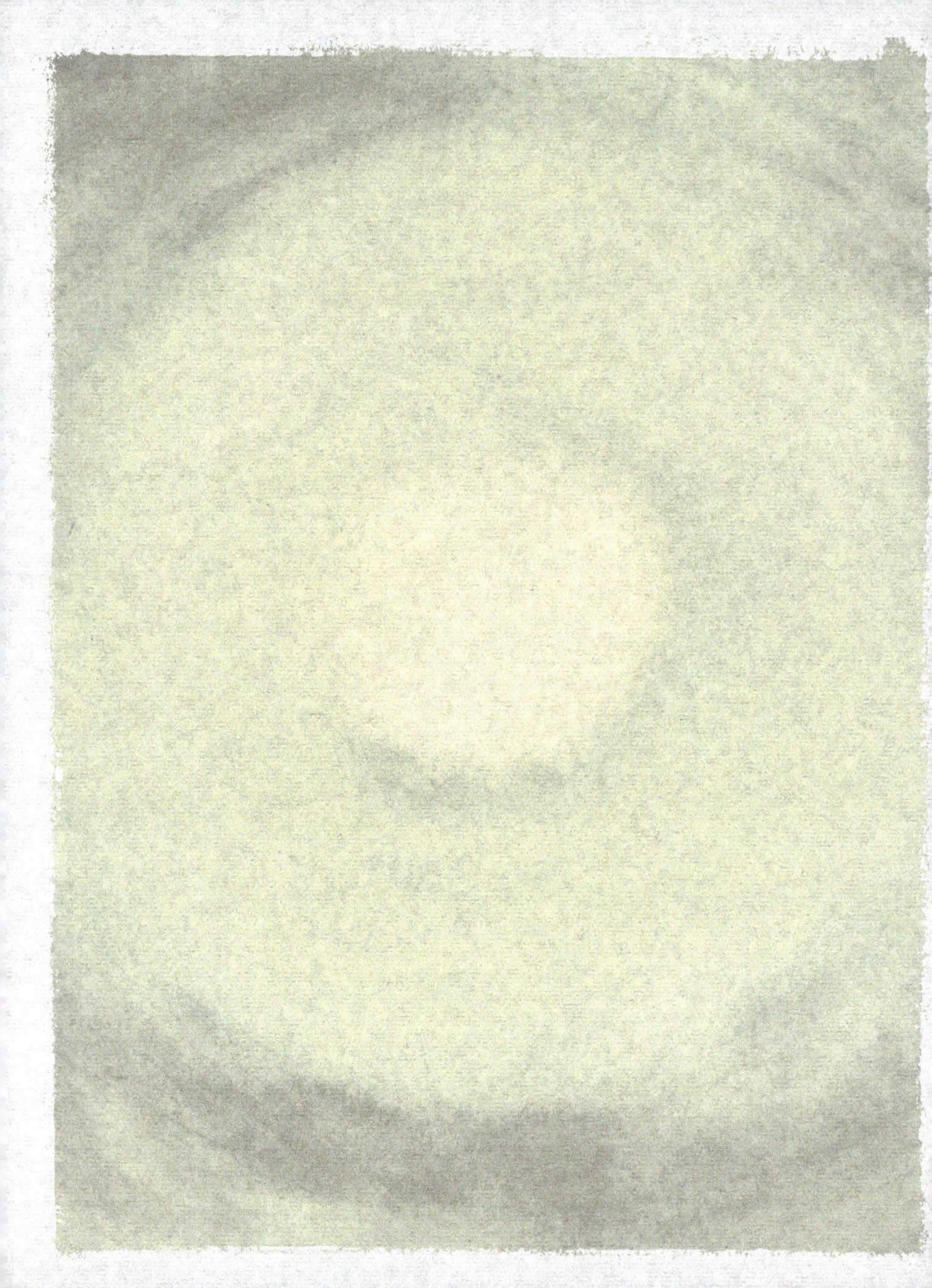

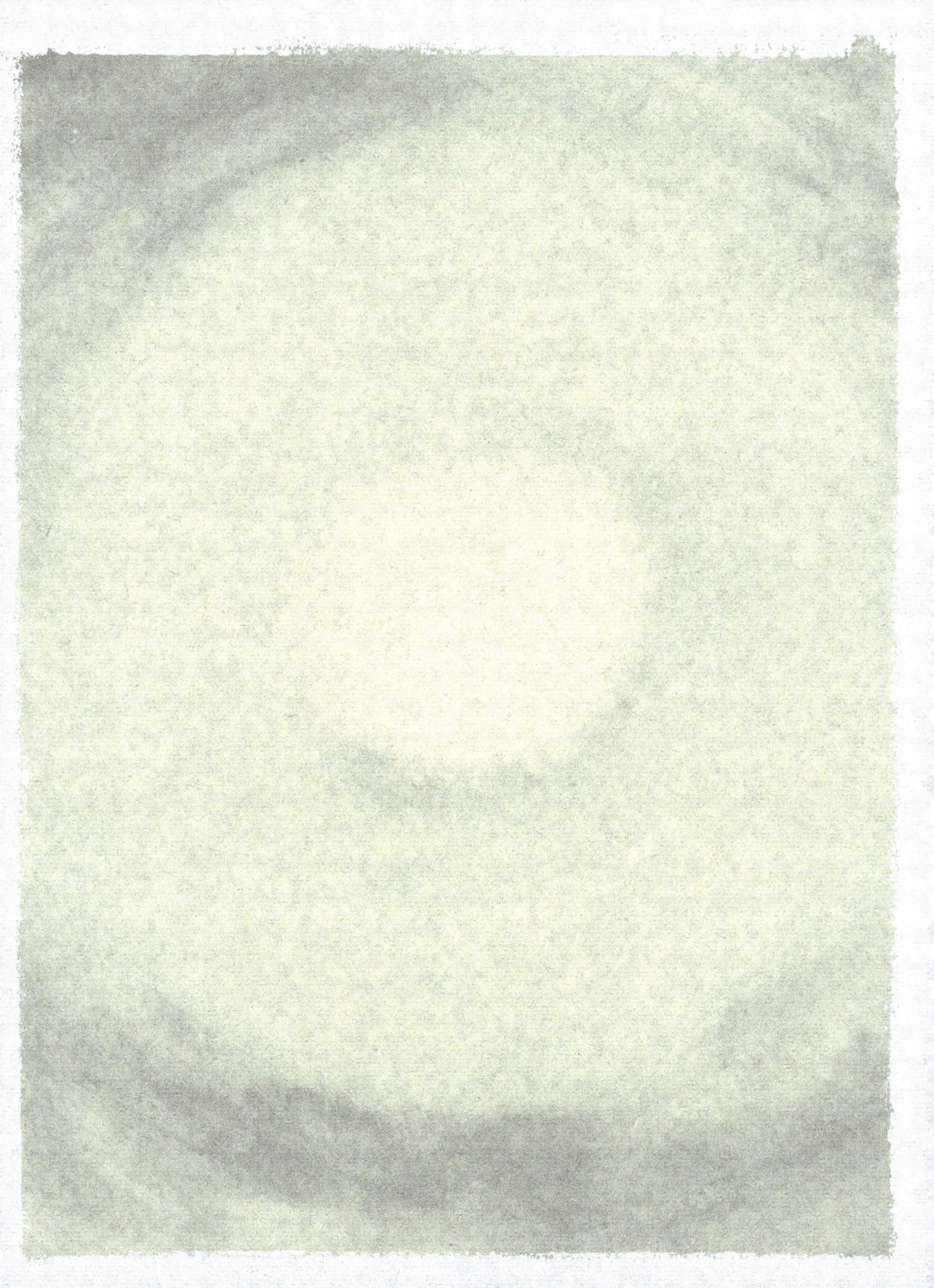

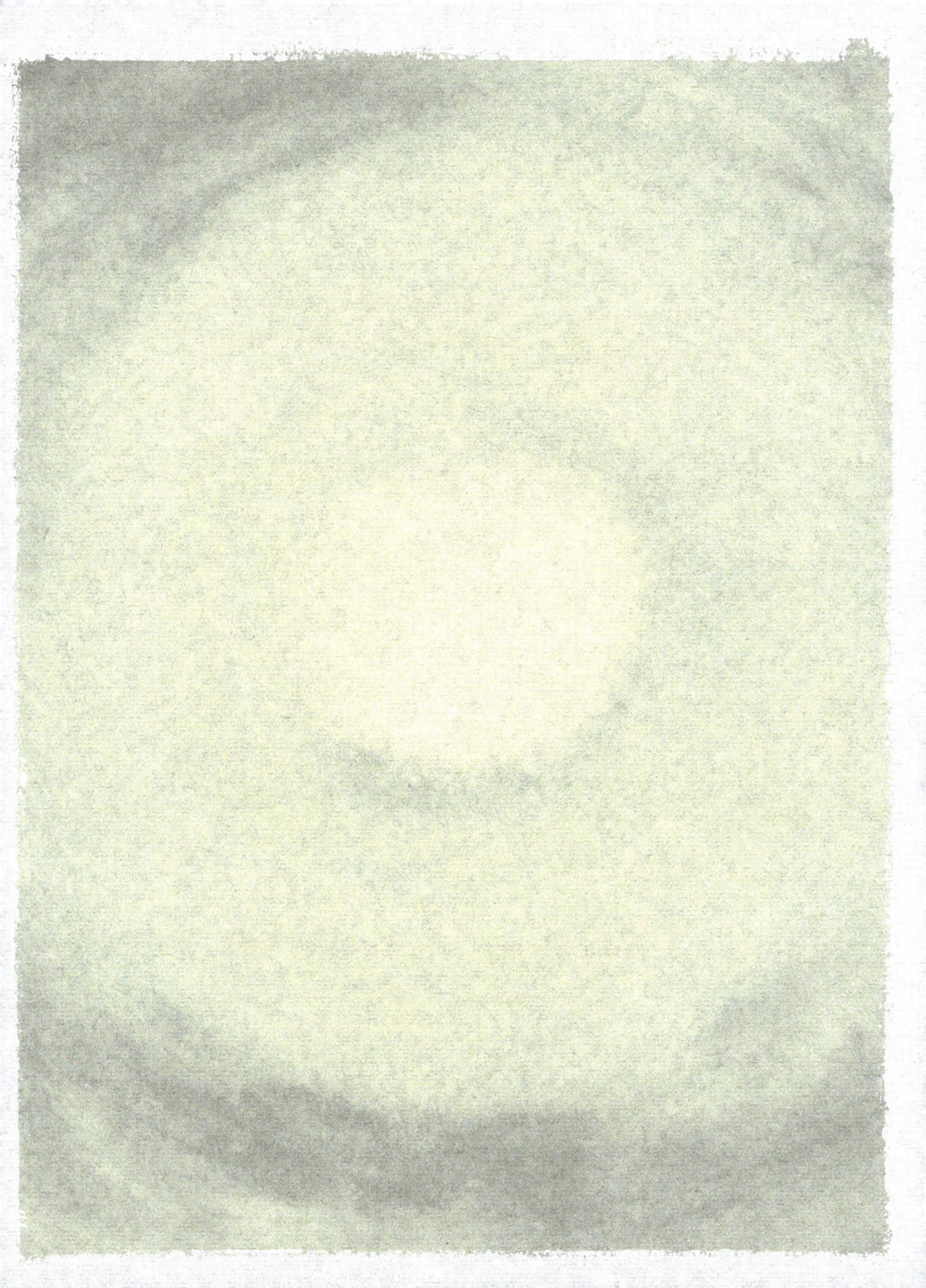

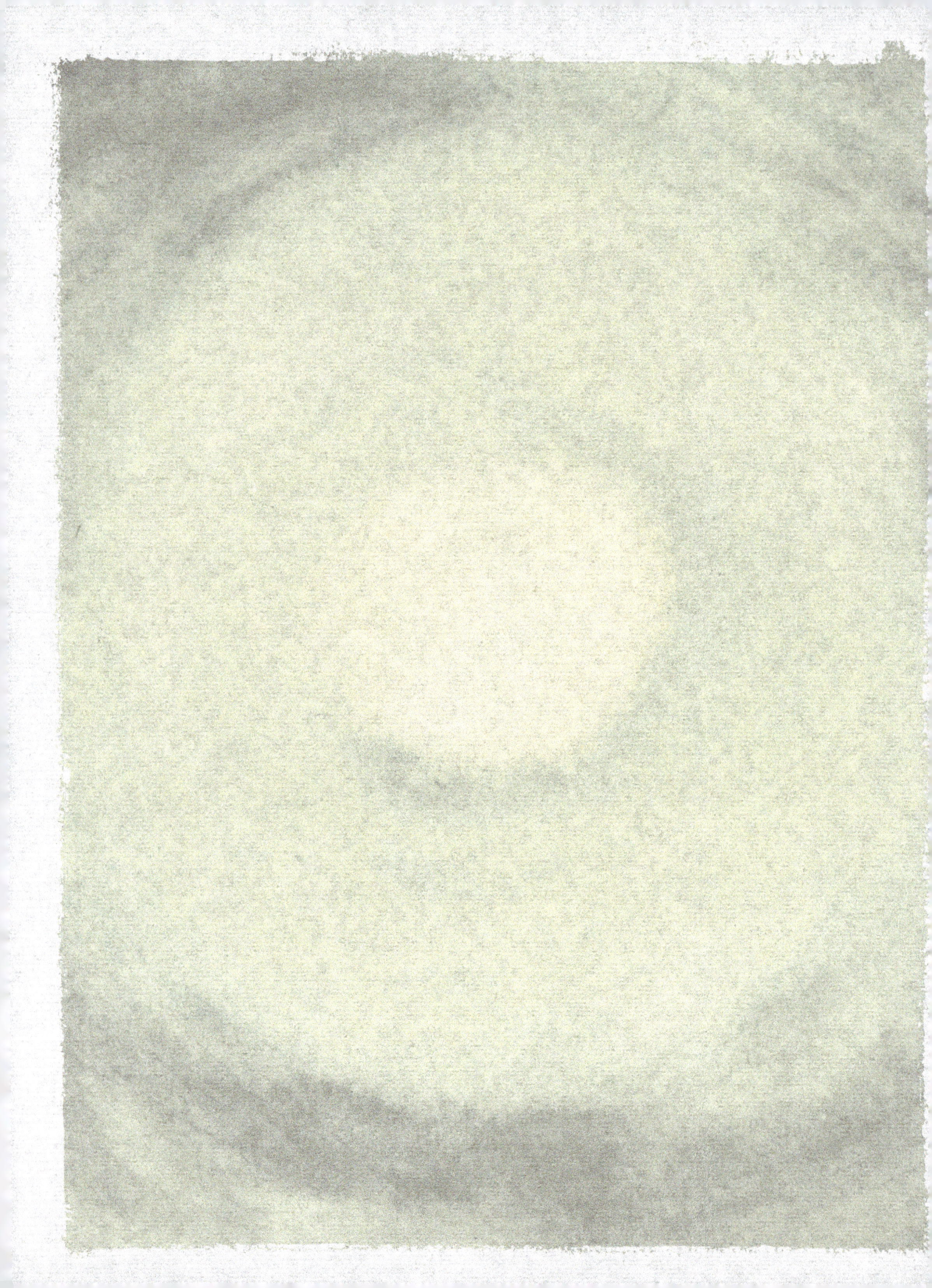

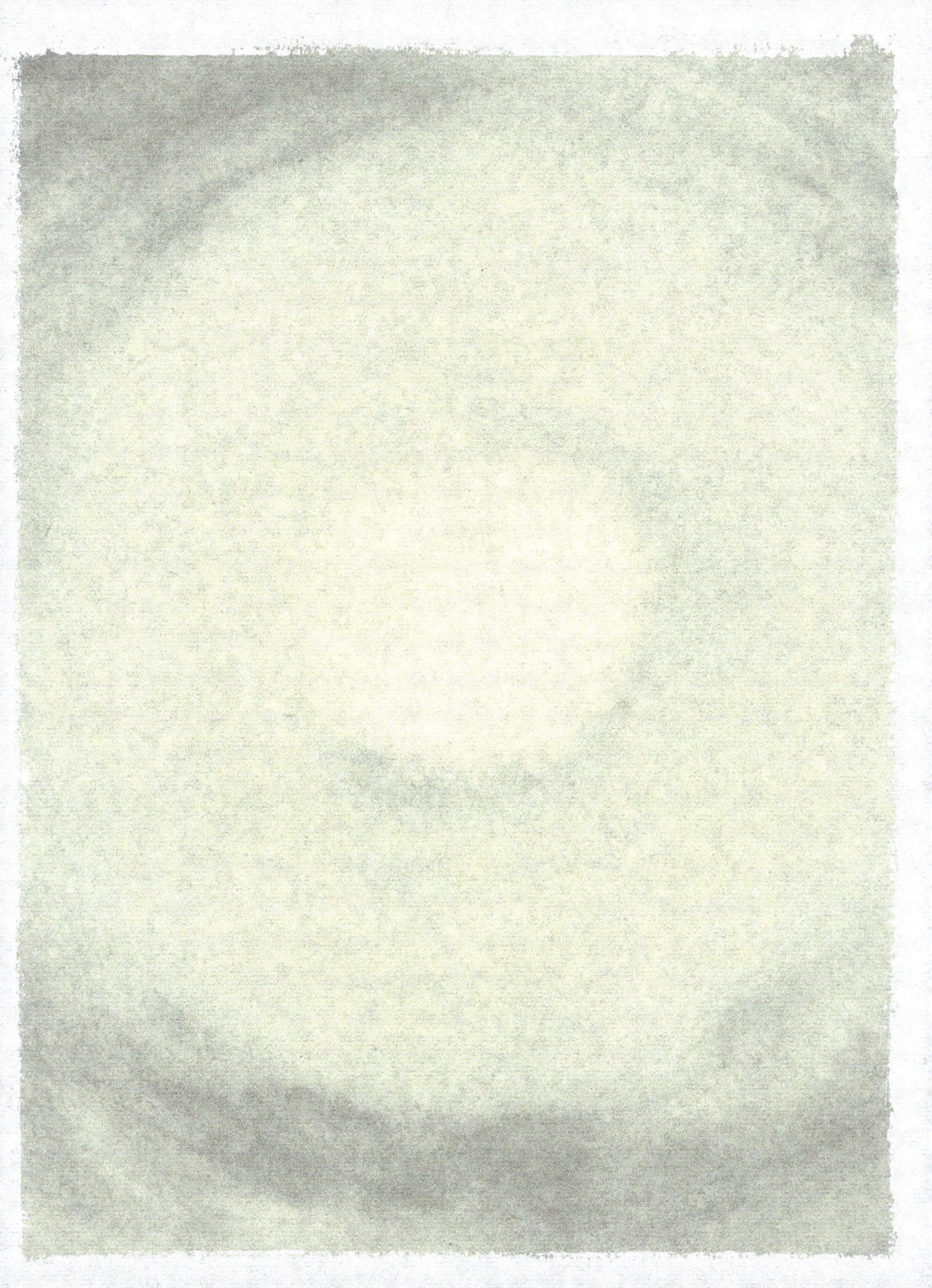

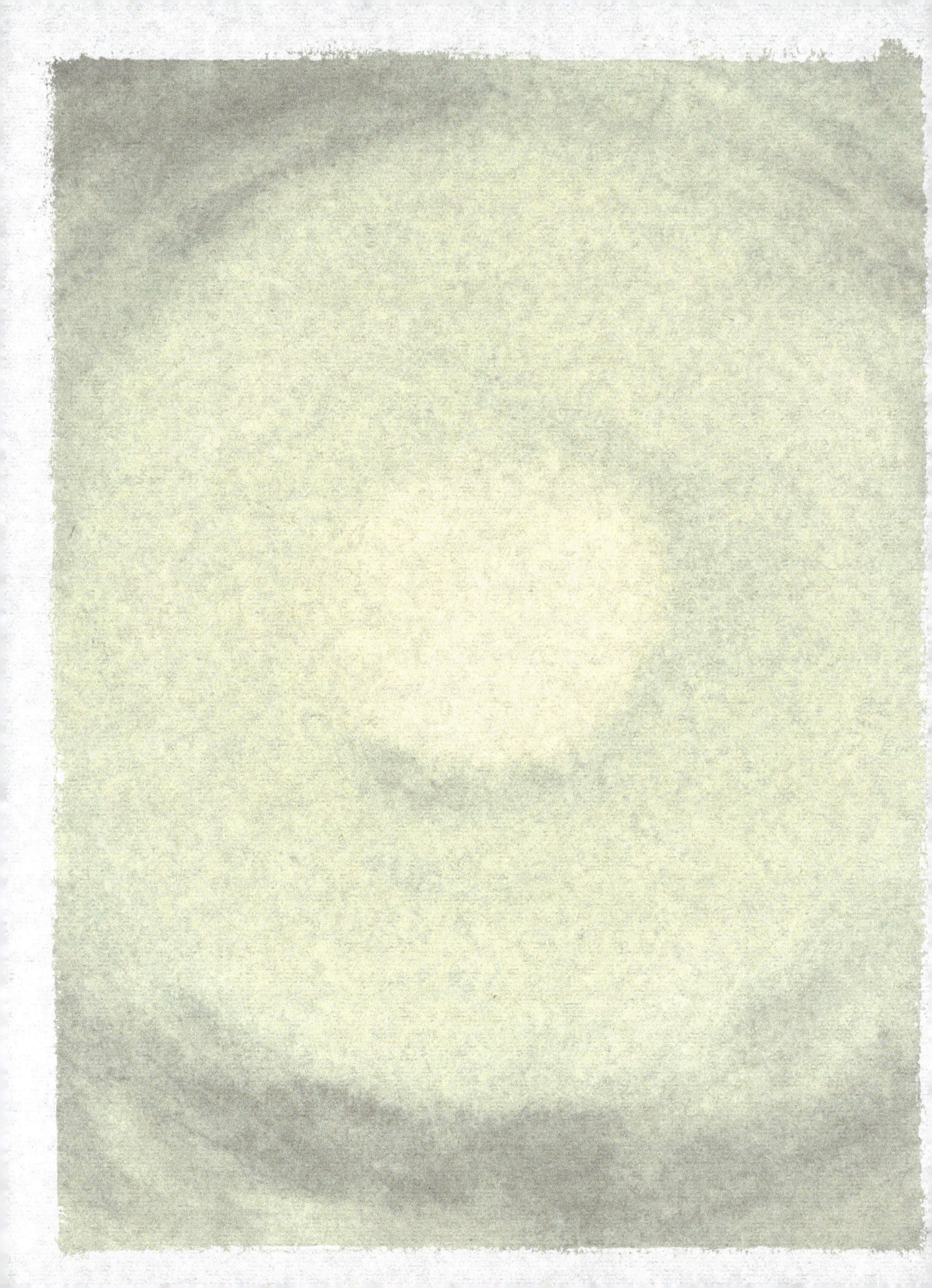

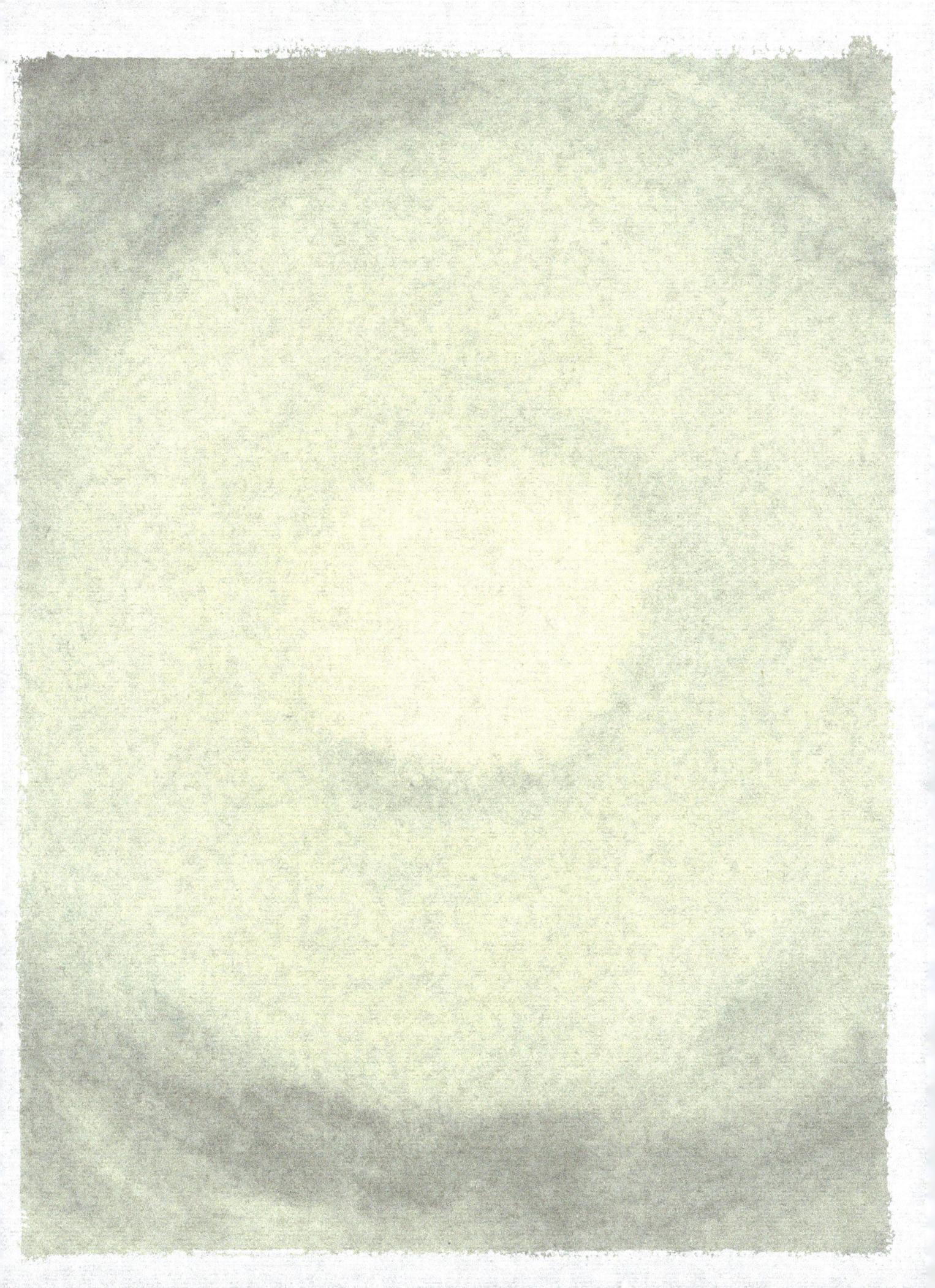

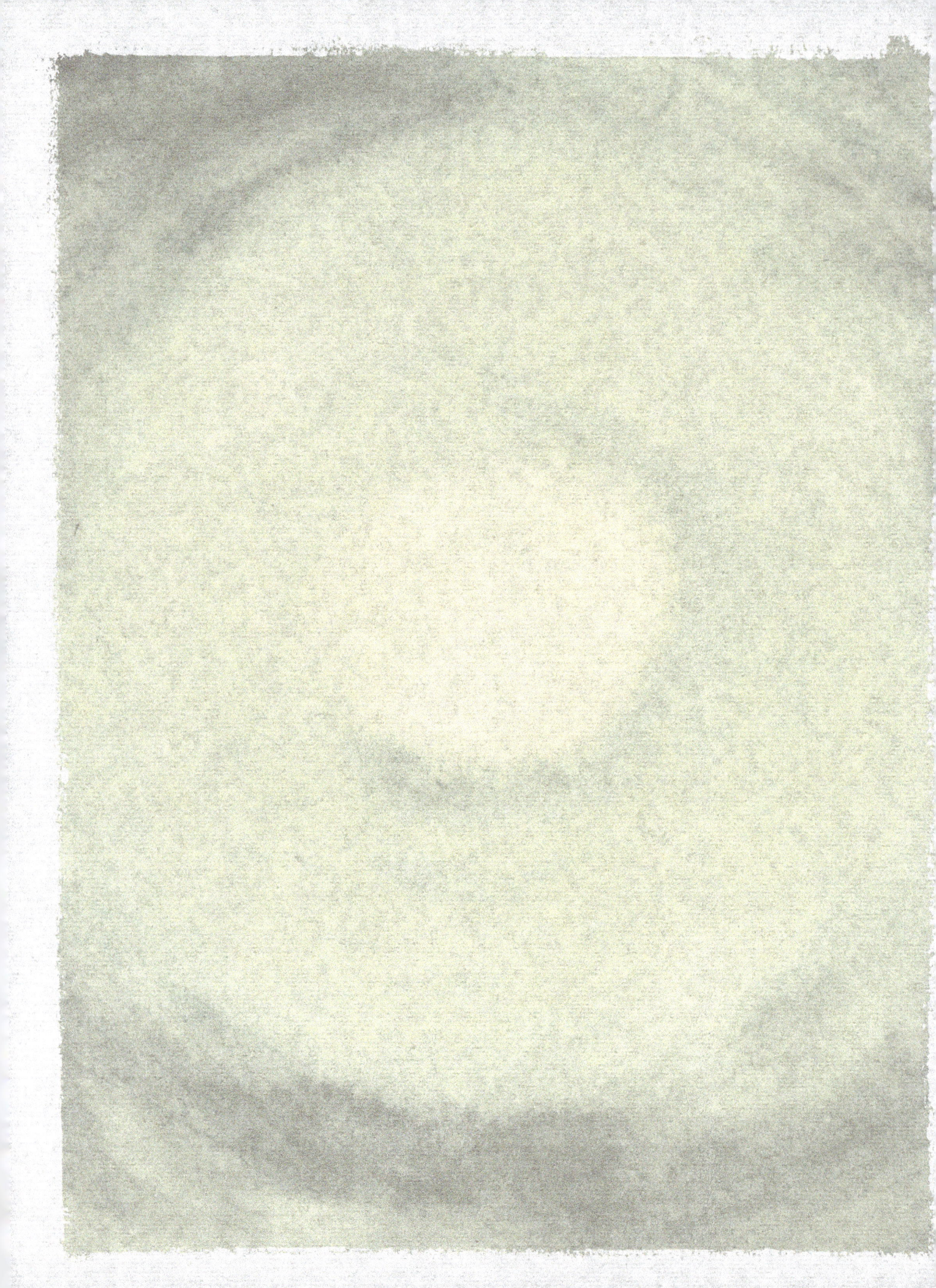

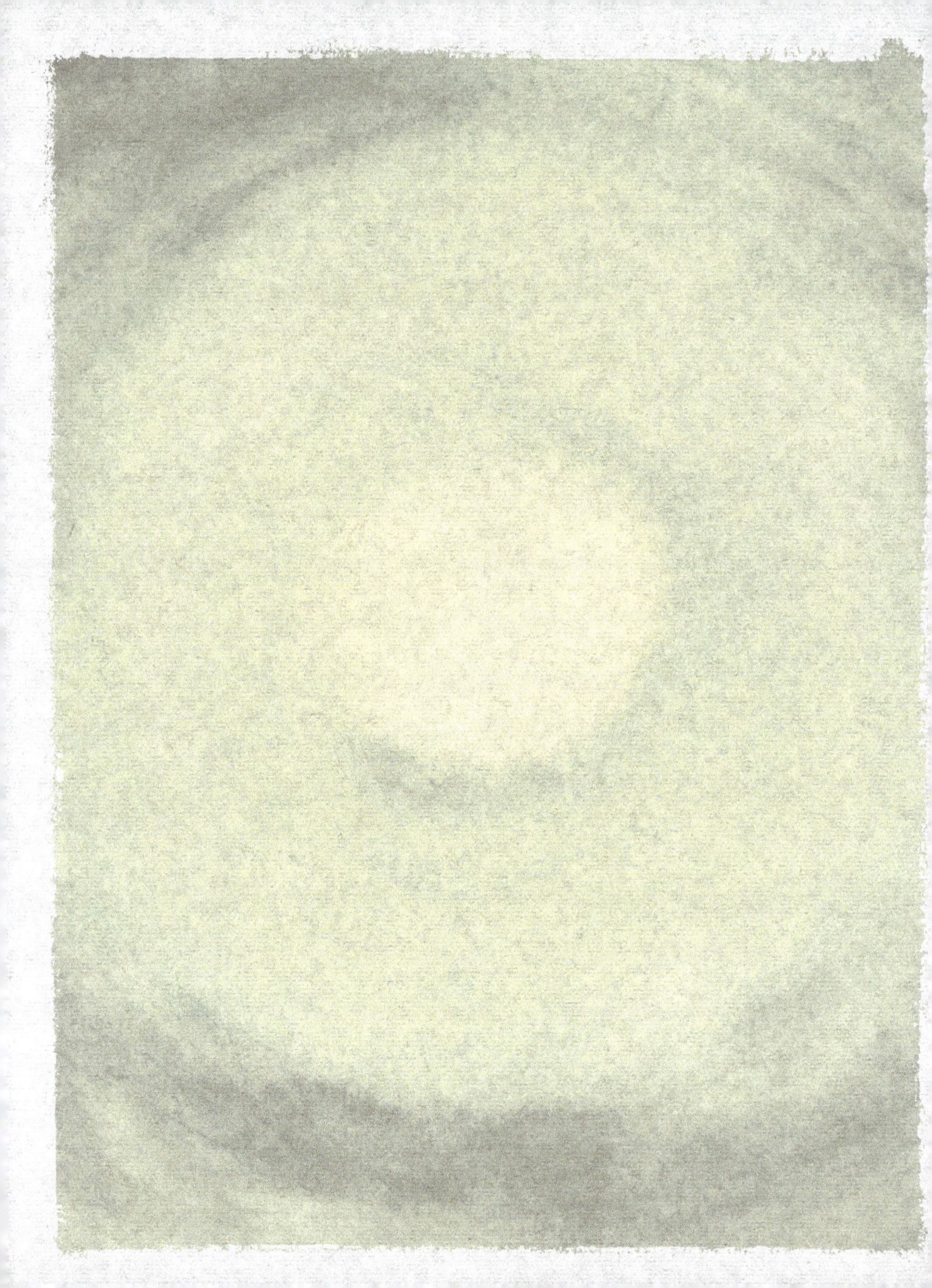

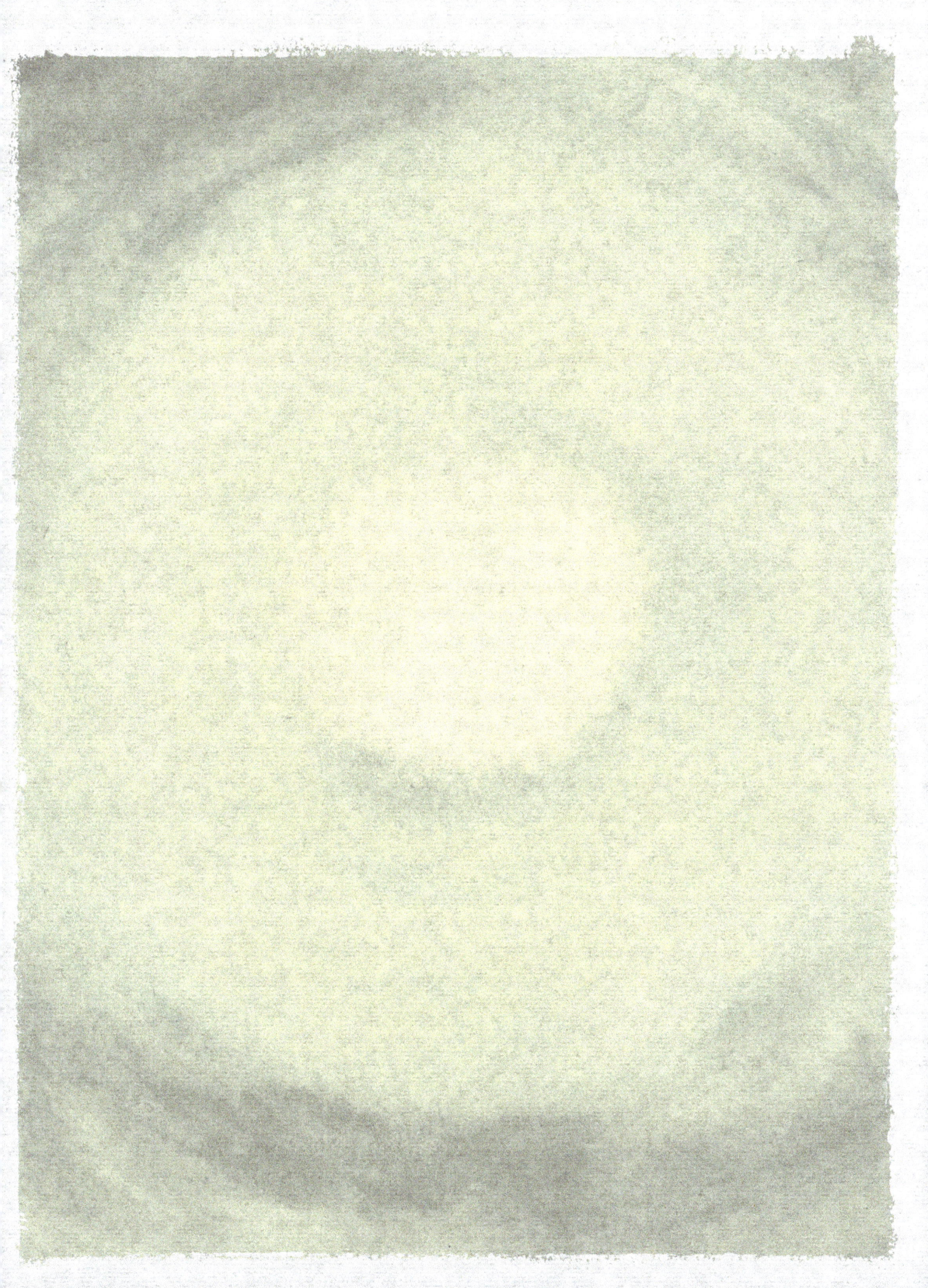

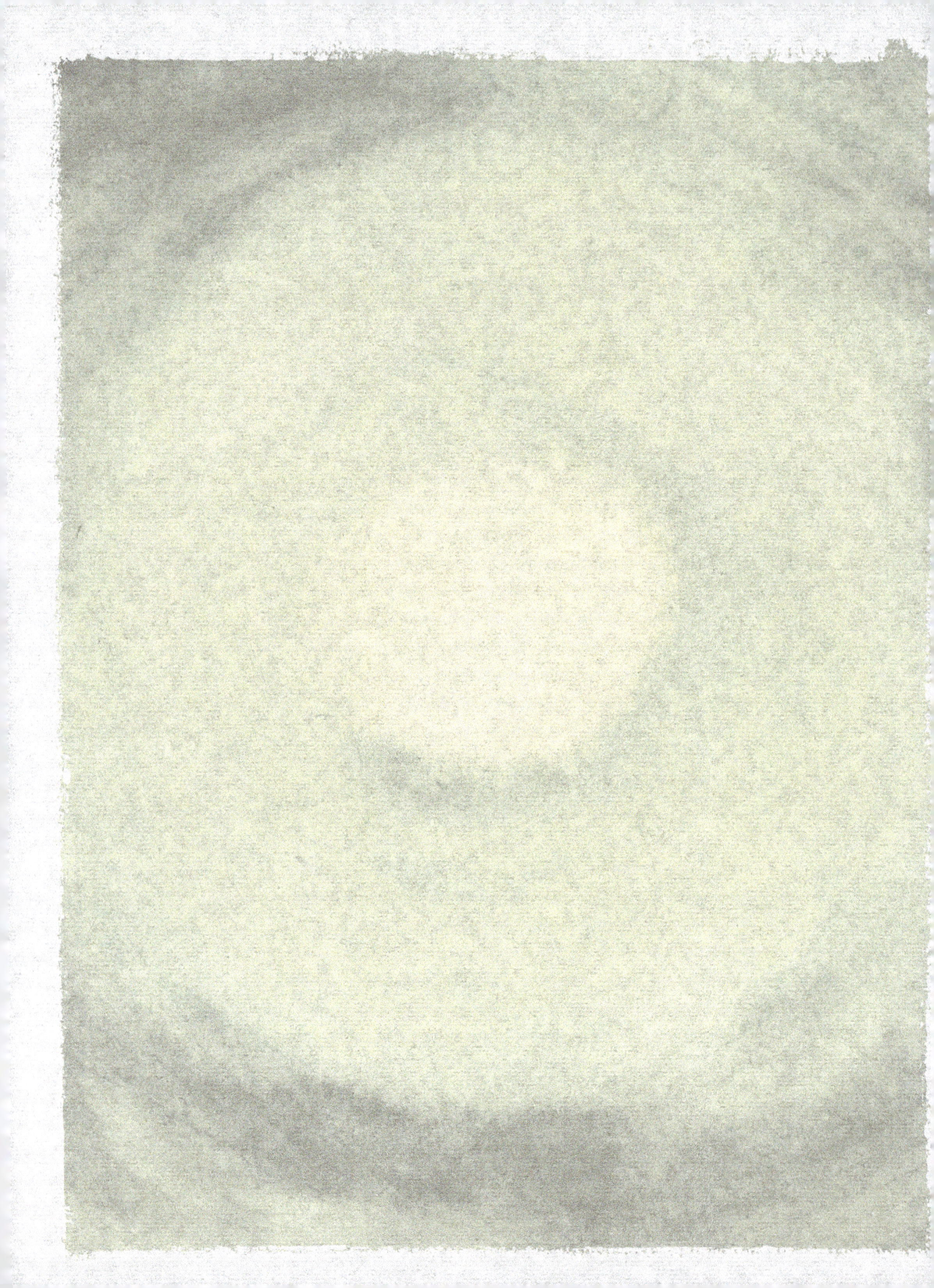

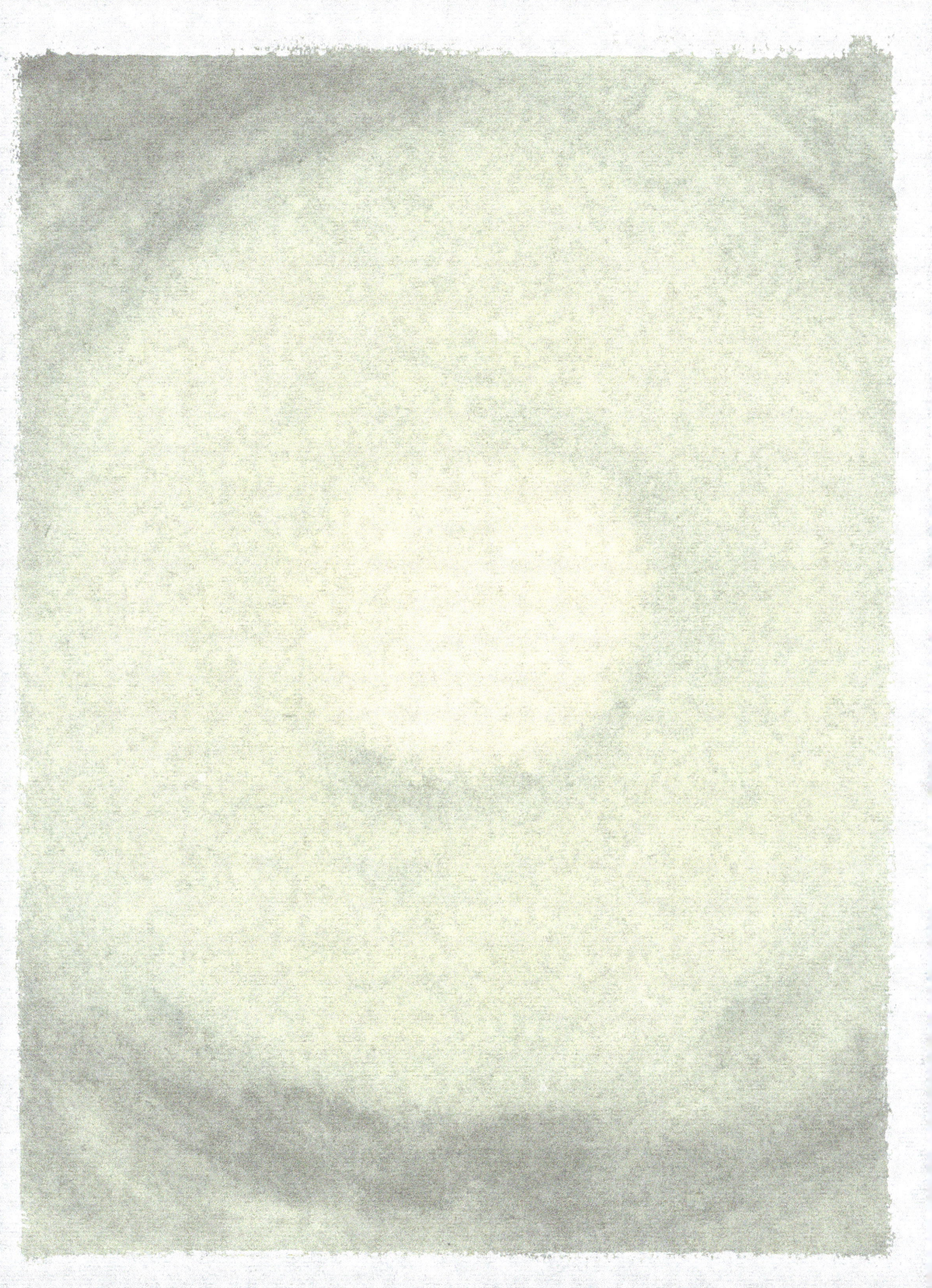

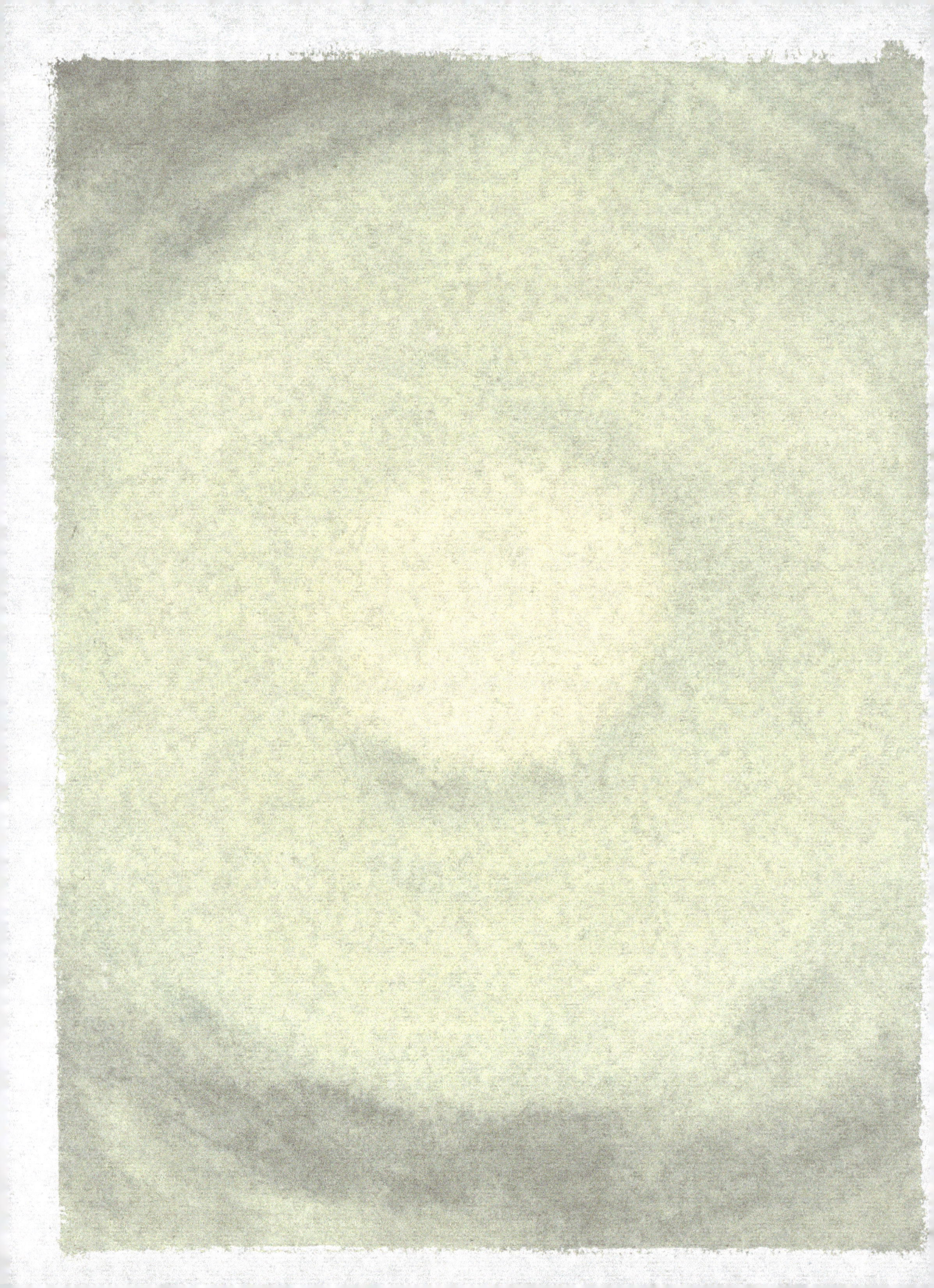

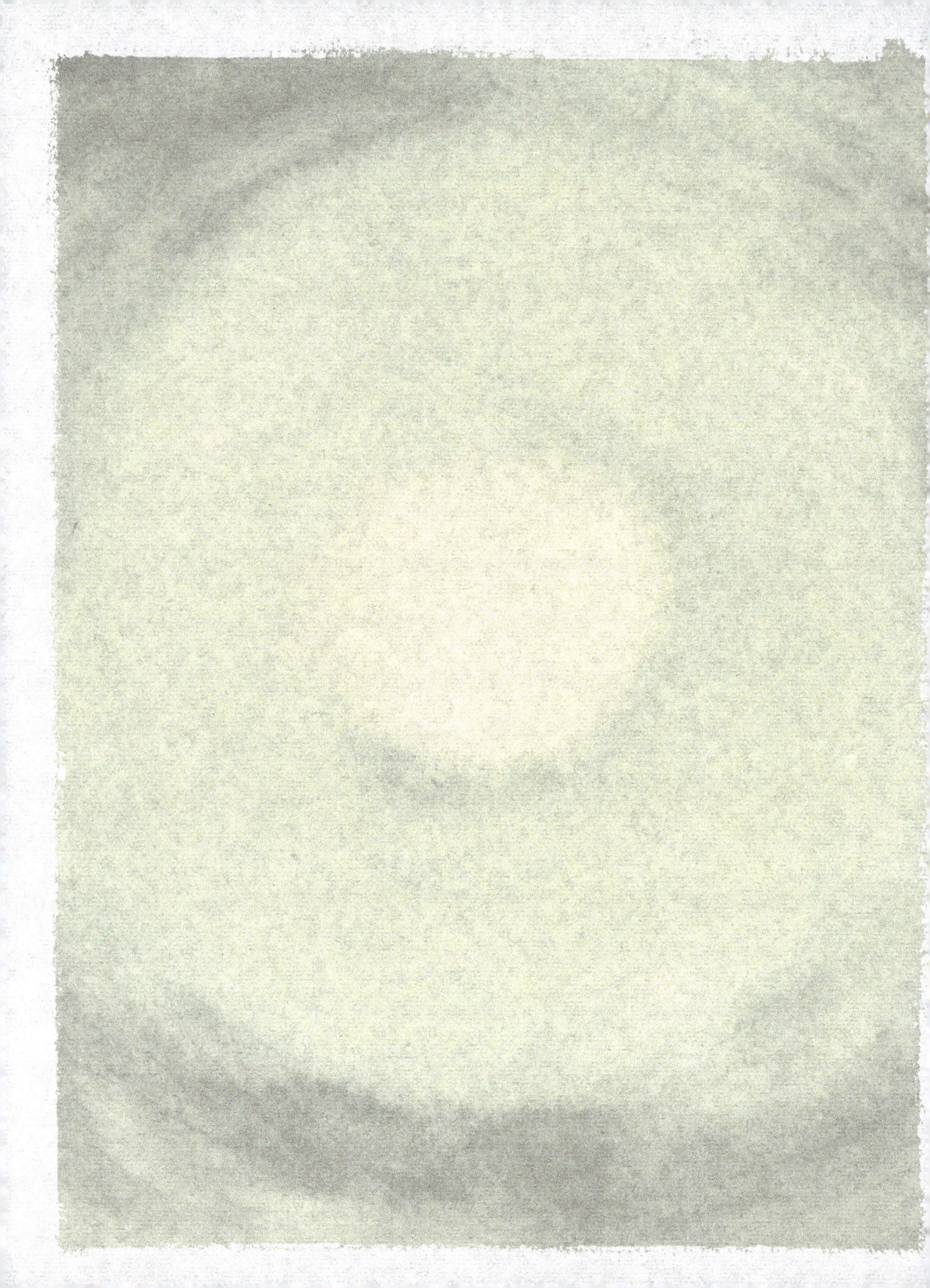

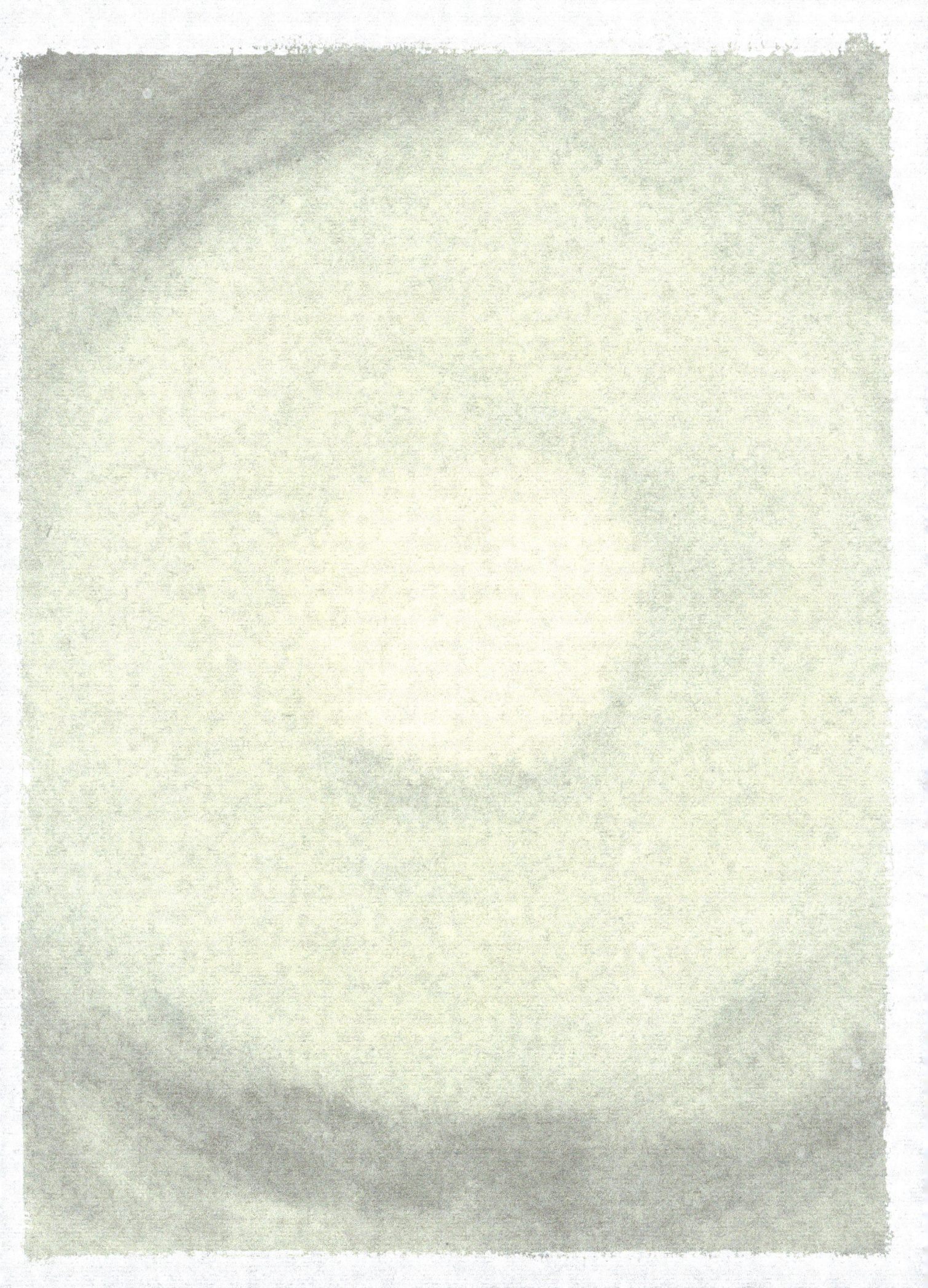

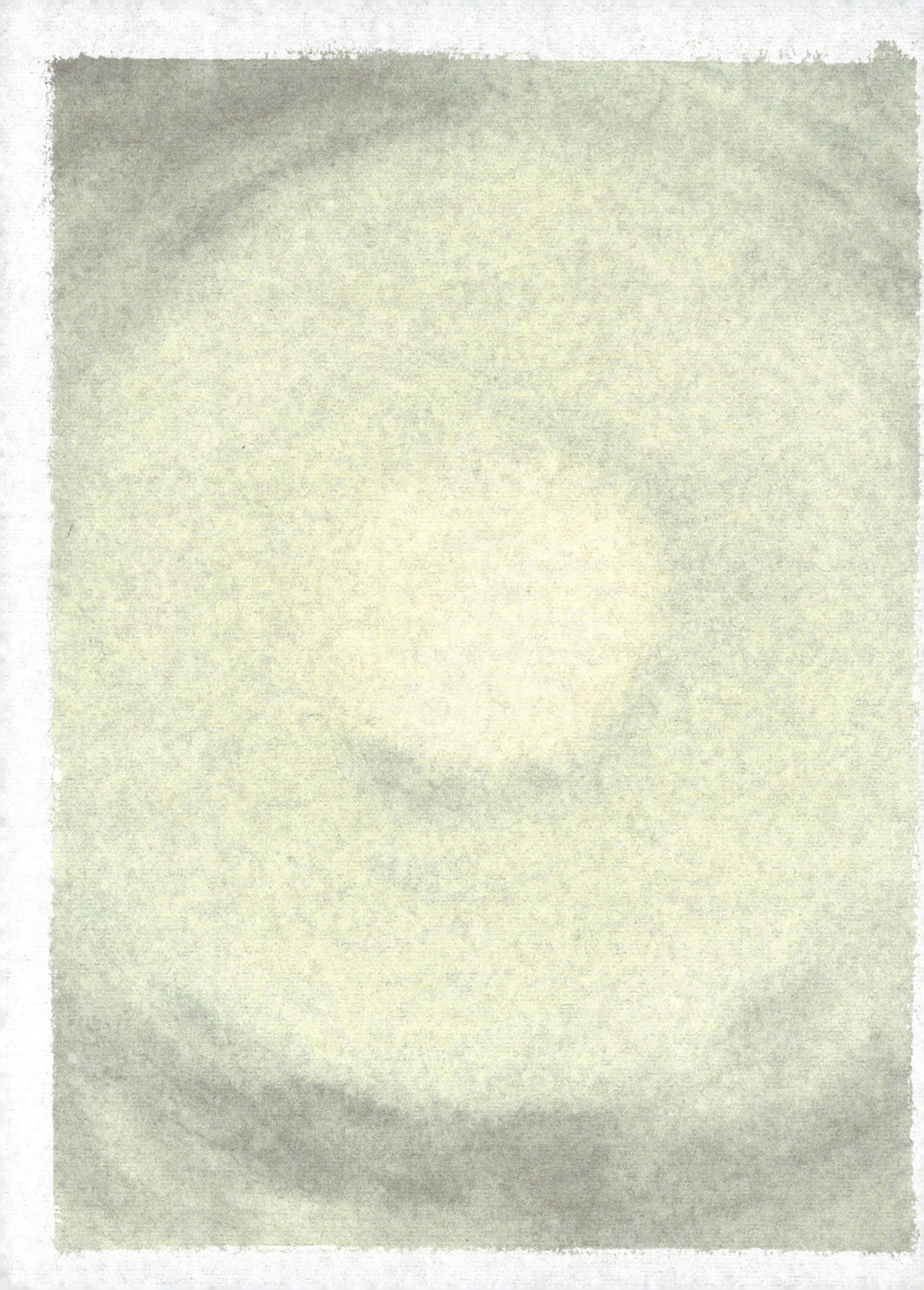

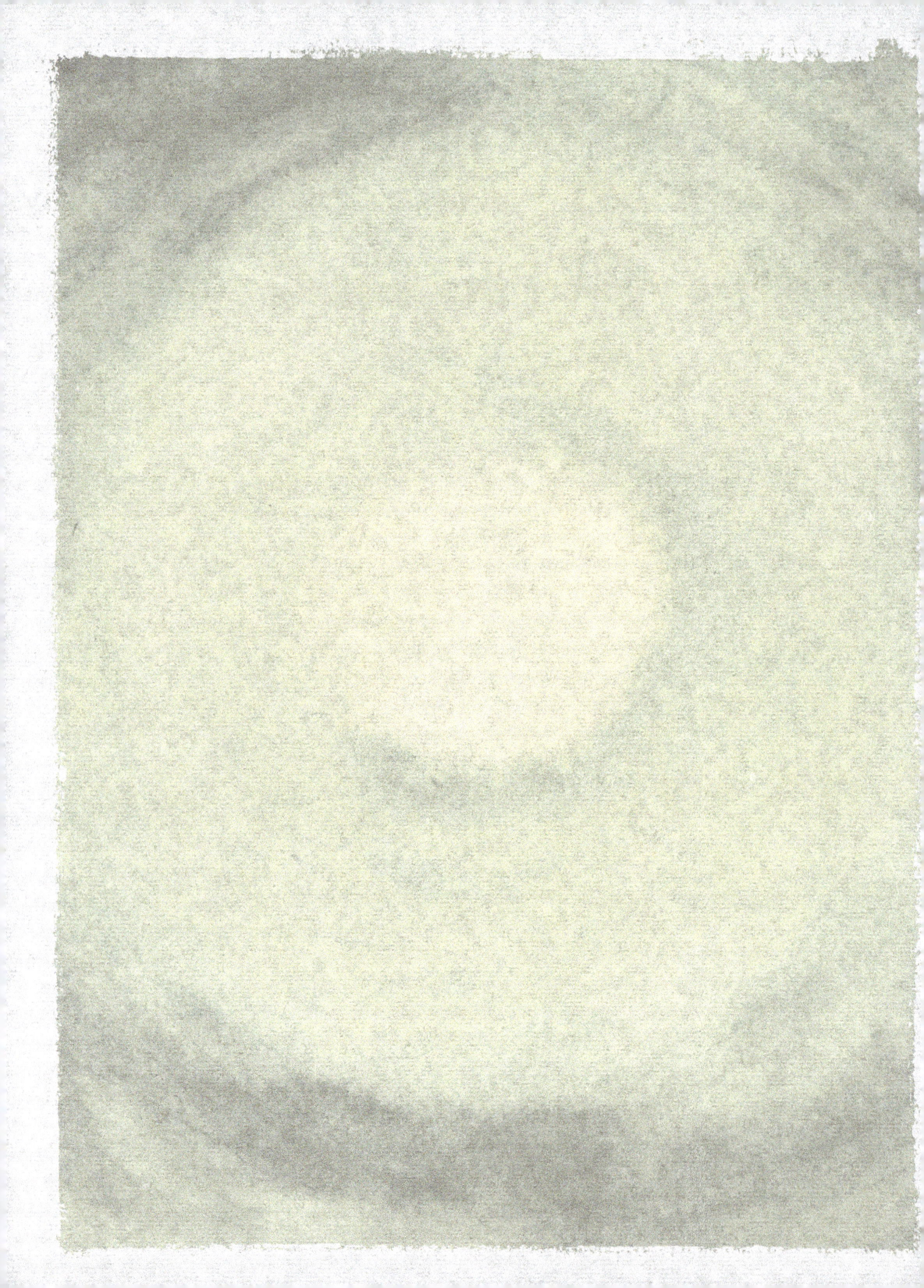

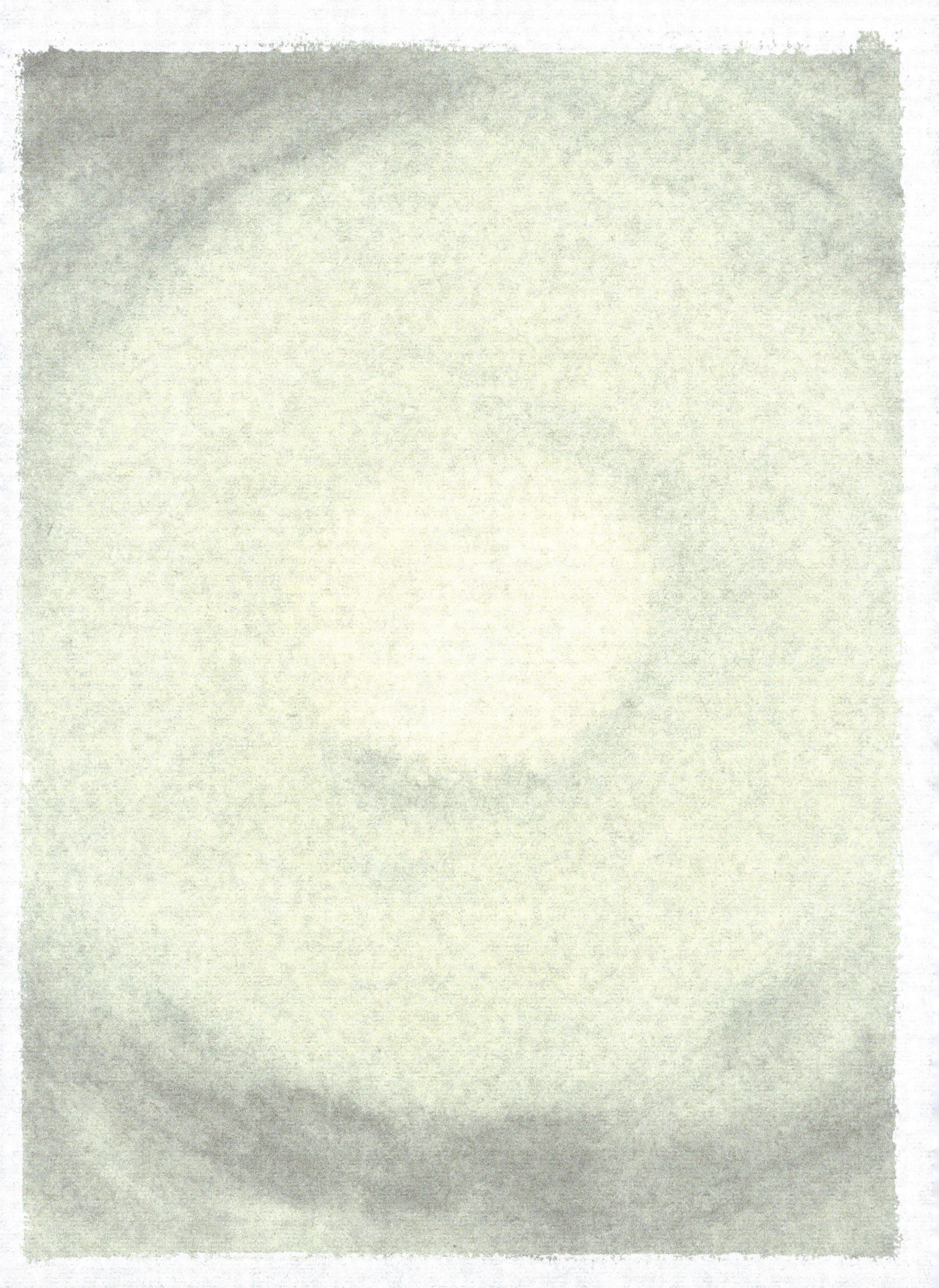

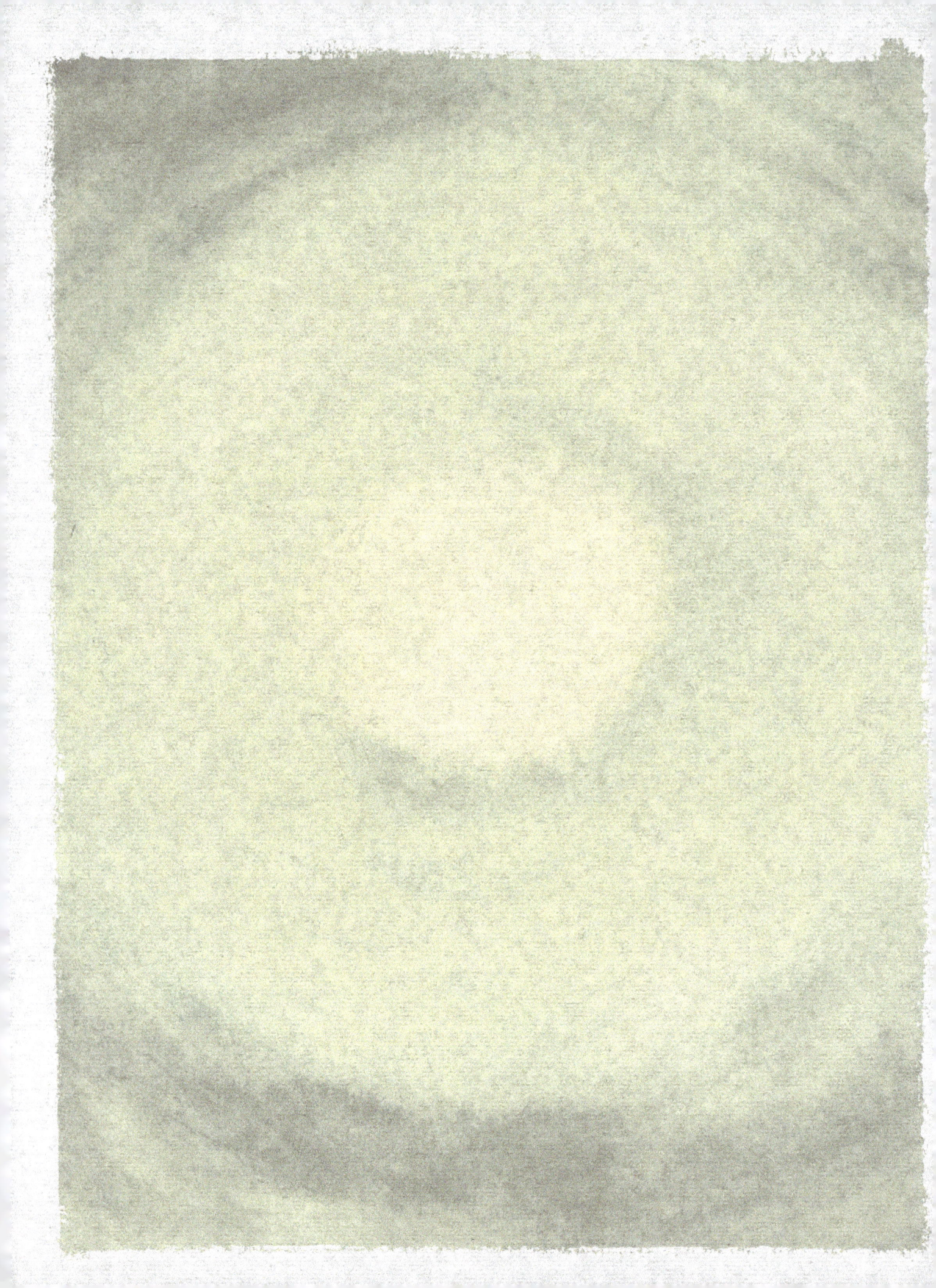

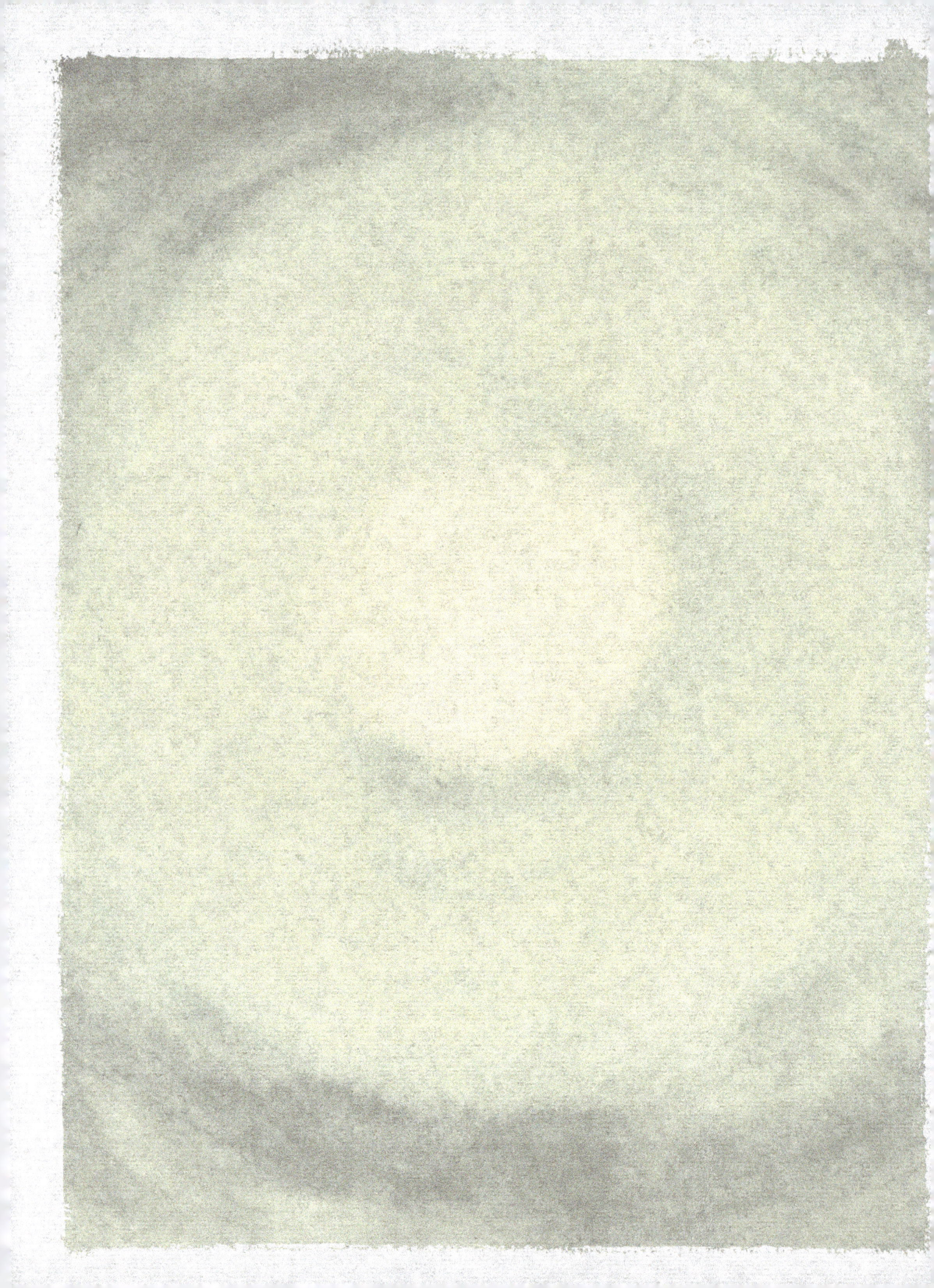

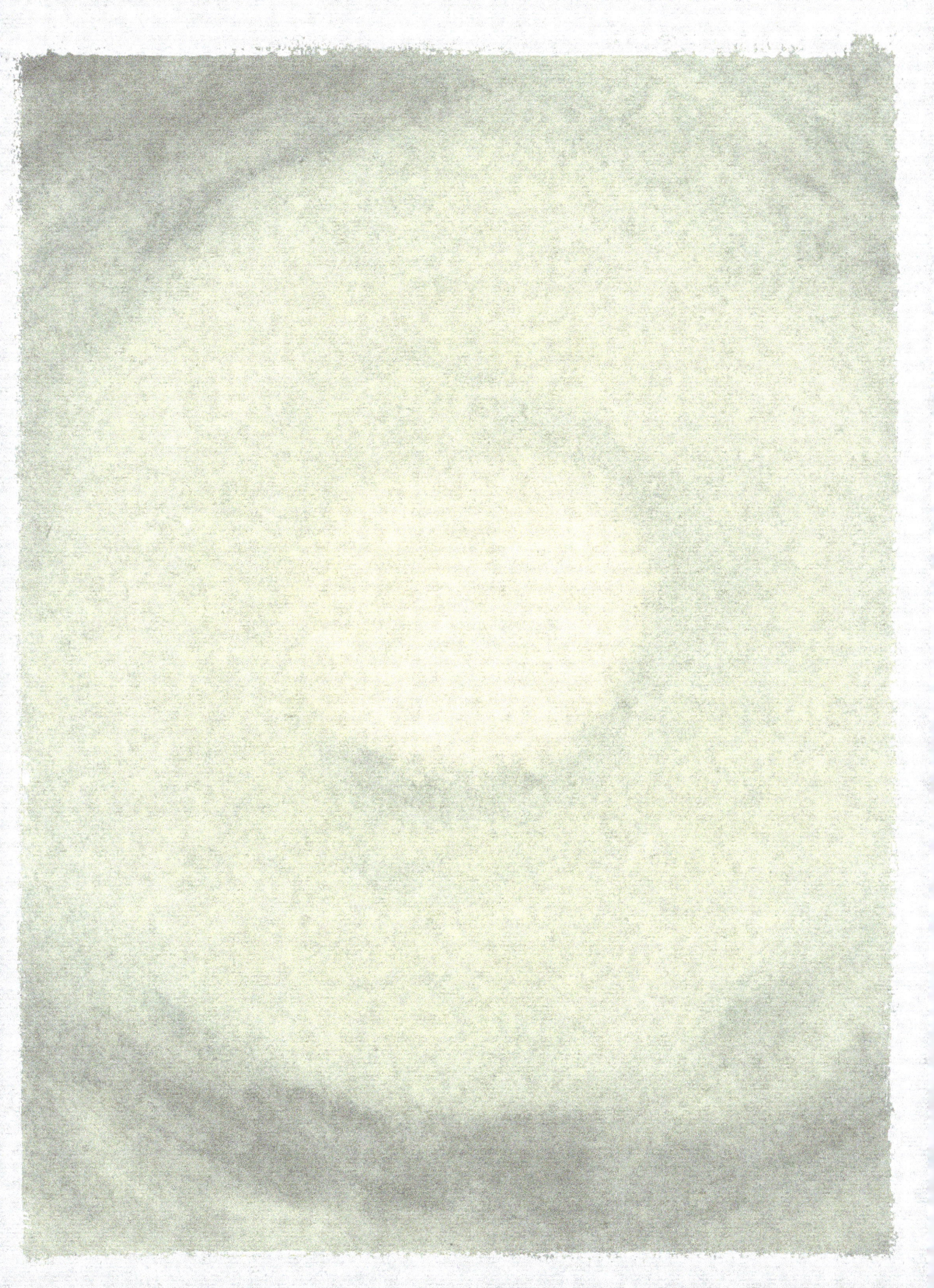

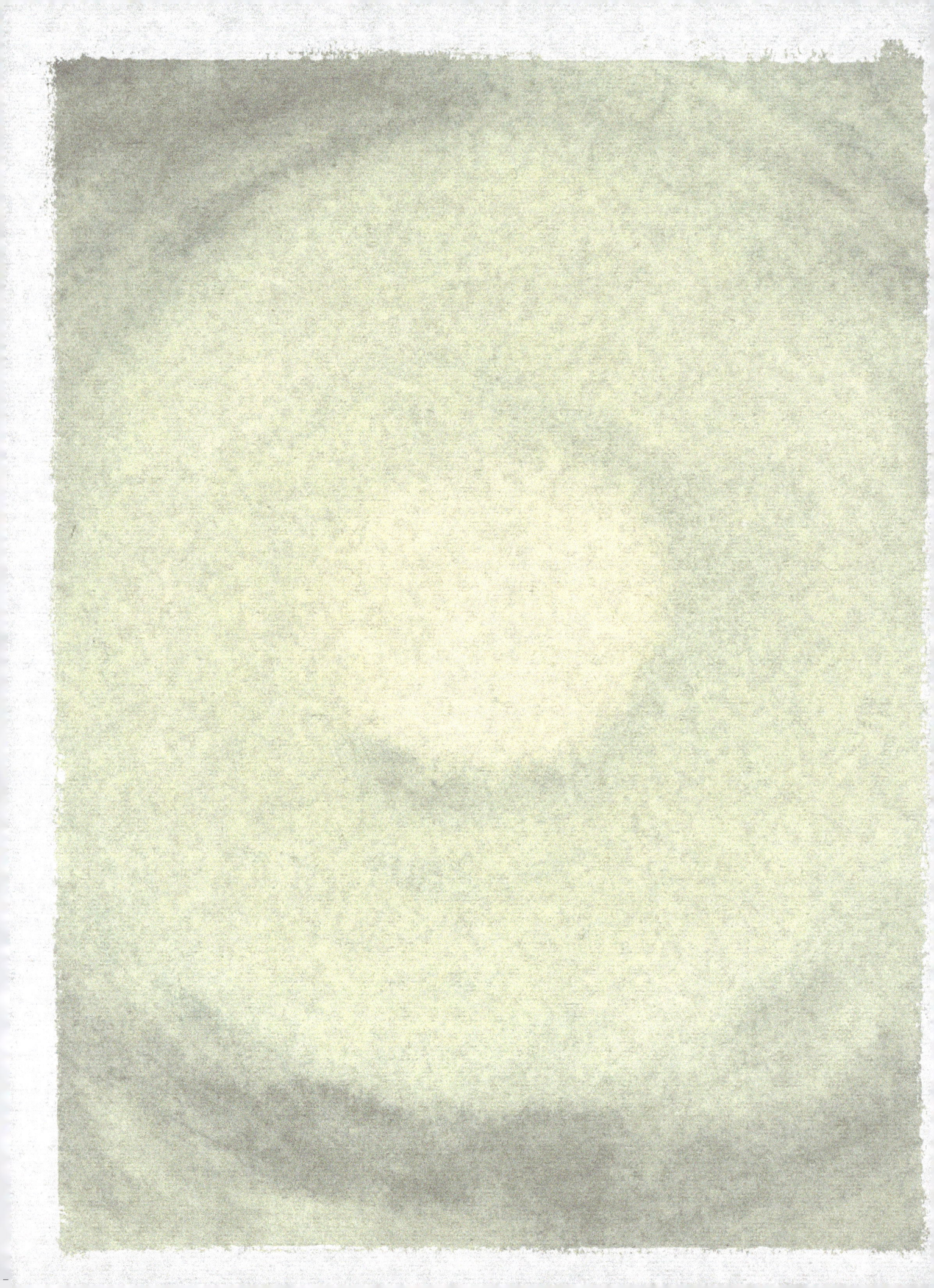

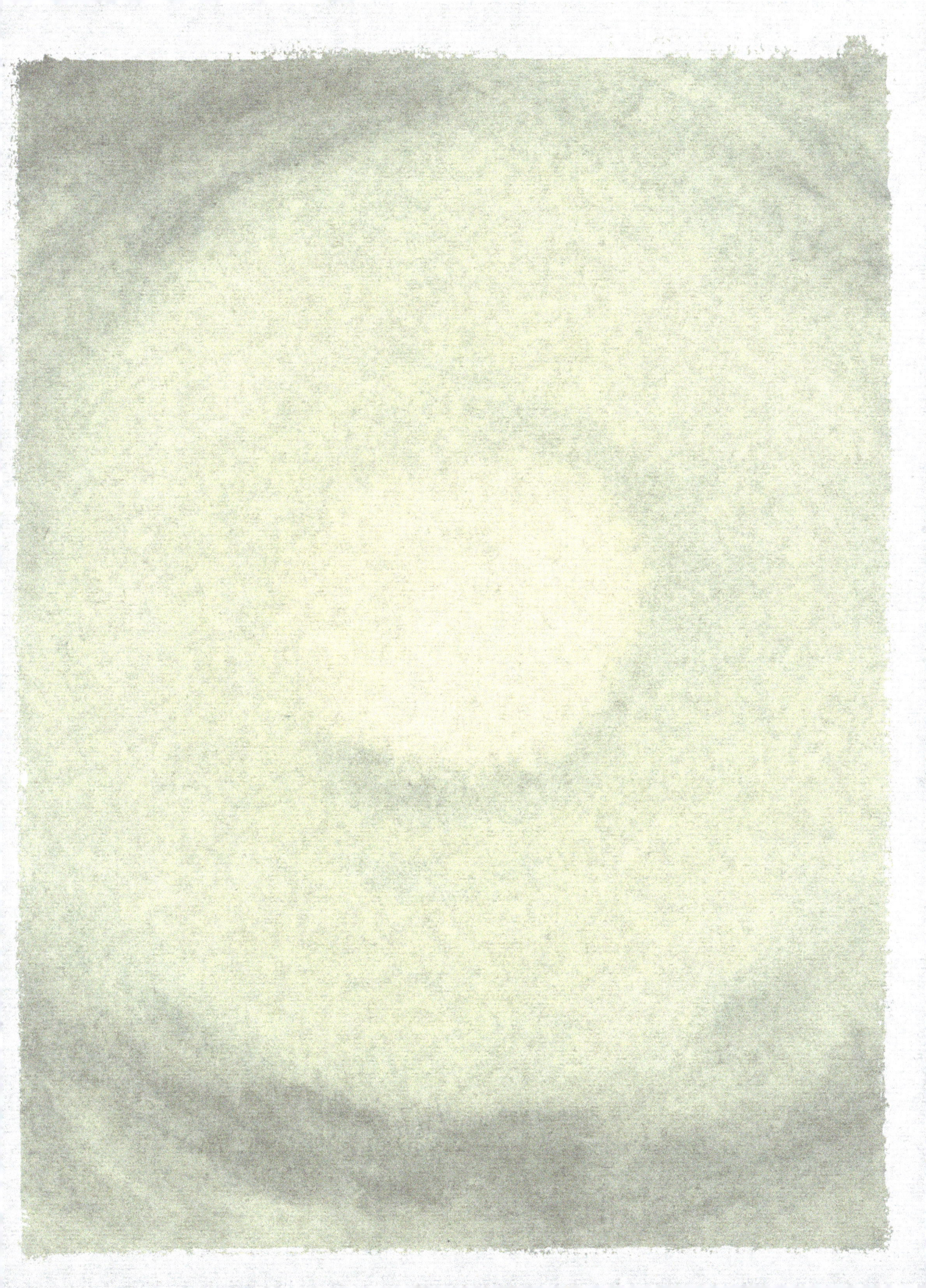

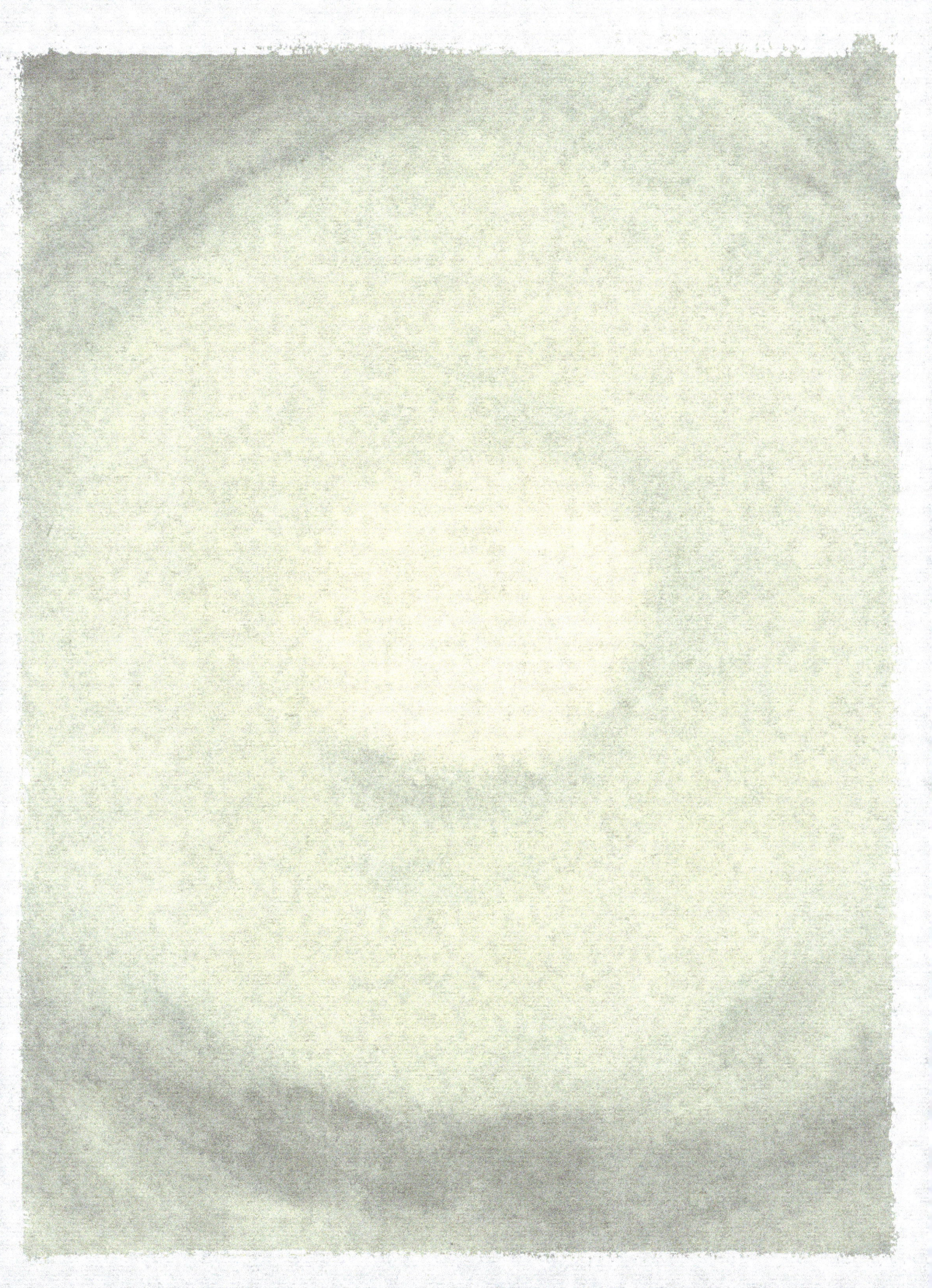

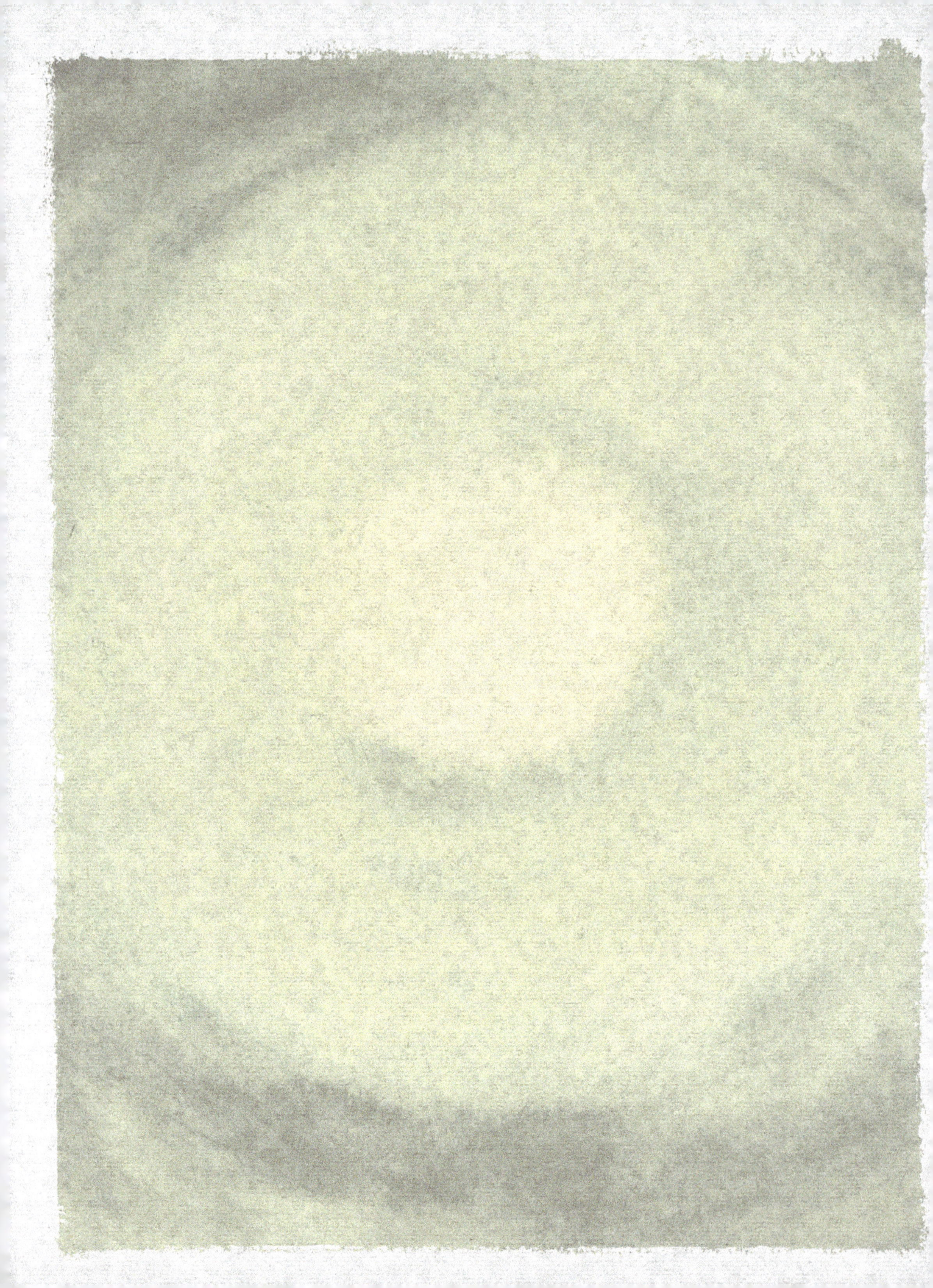

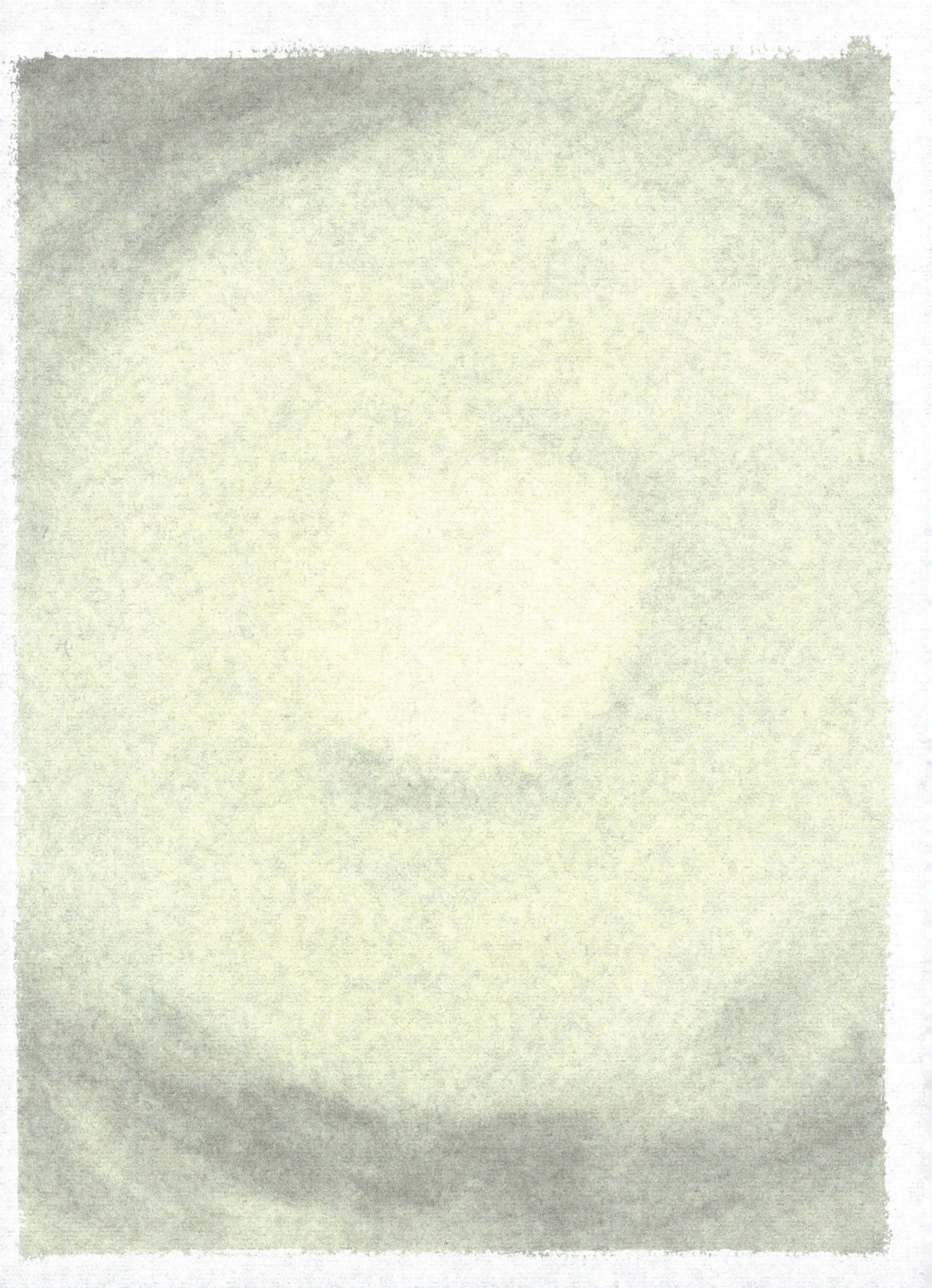

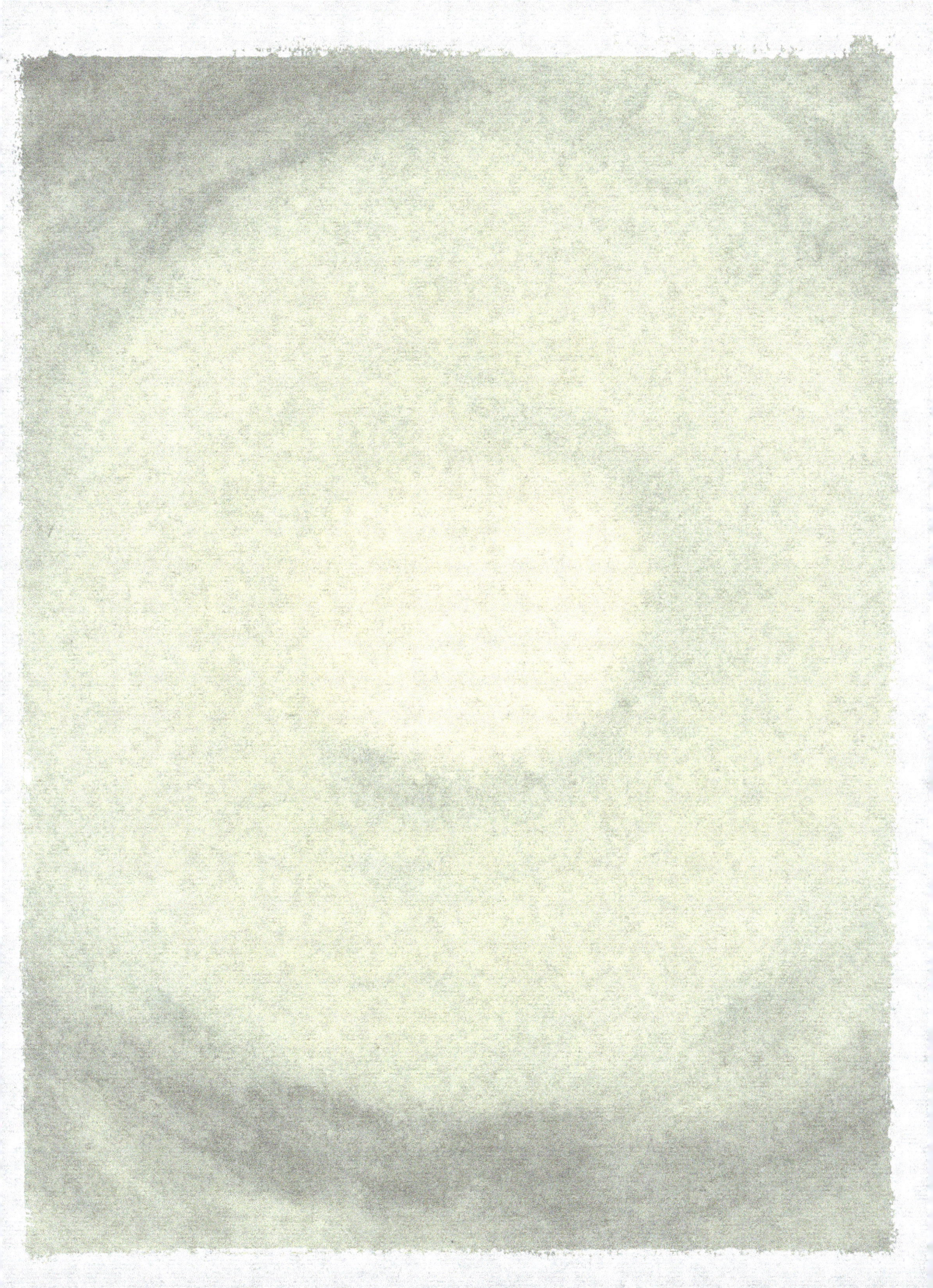

ABOUT the CREATOR

Annette Bridges is an author, publisher and women's retreat host on a mission to help every woman realize her story is extraordinary, valuable and noteworthy.

She has published the *Color Your World Journal Series* and formed a journal club to provide community, support and tools for women to record their ideas, feelings, experiences, memories and all the important details of their lives.

Before writing books and publishing journals and coloring books, this former public school and homeschool educator spent a decade writing hundreds of helpful, instructive, and light-hearted columns published by Texas newspapers, parenting magazines, websites and bloggers.

Annette lives on a Texas cattle ranch with her husband John, dachshund Lady and lots of cows. She can drive a tractor but only if wearing a fresh coat of lipstick and it's not her pedicure day!

You can learn more about Annette's books and products, blogs and videos as well as her women's retreats and other events at www.annettebridges.com.

Look for her on social media, too!

MESSAGE from the PUBLISHER

The **Color Your World Journal Series** is a pathway to self-discovery. It's where you write notes to yourself. Be your own cheerleader. Give yourself encouragement. Tell yourself what you're grateful for. Celebrate you!

There are countless reasons to keep a journal including collecting favorite recipes, listing goals and celebrating every experience and every one that's near and dear to you. A journal provides a home for the memories and lessons learned that you never want to forget.

Why a niche journal?

If you're anything like me, you have a journal (or even two or three journals) where you write anything and everything about anything and everything. My challenge comes when trying to find something I've written. I flip and flip through the pages of my two, three or four journals trying to find whatever it is. I never remember which journal I wrote down my whatever's!!

The solution? A niche journal! A journal that has a specific focus and theme! A journal where you can record your ideas, inspirations and things you want to remember in the appropriate journal.

Why big unlined paper?

Because big unlined paper is needed to record big ideas, dreams and memories! You need room to grow, stretch and expand. You need space to think beyond the confines of what you've always done, to pursue new dreams, discover your power and reimagine your purpose again and again. You need pages without lines and limitations to reconnect with your creative, perfectly imperfect self.

Plus, big unlined paper gives you space for more than words. You have plenty of room to doodle, draw or post photographs and clippings, too.

Why color is important?

When you journal, use colored pens and markers! Your world doesn't happen in black and white. Your life should be lived and written about in many colors. Even dark and sad memories feel lighter and brighter when told in color.

Journaling in color affects your mood and perception of your world. Colors evoke calm, cheer and comfort. Using color can lift your spirit and inspire your imagination. You may be surprised by all the beautiful benefits from adding more color into your life story.

When journaling, give yourself time to listen to your heart and reflect. Breathe in the moments. Feel. Be quiet. Let yourself be totally and thoroughly present with your thoughts. Let your heart transform you and teach you new insights. Open your mind to consider new ideas and possibilities. You may find that what your heart teaches will be life changing.

www.ingramcontent.com/pod-product-compliance
Lightning Source LLC
Chambersburg PA
CBHW051253110526
44588CB00025B/2972